The First World War Fact Book

1,568 facts on the war to end all wars

Scott Addington

Cover Image: Private John Hines with his trophies from the fighting at
Polygon Wood, Belgium.
AWM Negative E00822

For a fact on Private Hines, see the 'Combatants: ANZAC' section

CONTENTS

INTRODUCTION

Type in 'WW1 Fact book' or 'World War One Fact book' into Amazon and you are underwhelmed with choice. Until this book was published that is. Despite the thousands of books written on the subject, a simple fact book, one that is to the point, and easy to digest, seems to have been largely overlooked.

In an effort to fill this void, here is my attempt at a fact book on the First World War. I have tried to cover all the major areas of the war in separate sections, I hope that this gives an elements of structure to a project that could easily become a bit of a monster!

The facts in this book have come from many different sources, a list of references can be found at the end. With complicated events such as world wars, there can be many different variations and interpretations of the same event or fact. For example casualty rates can vary wildly depending on which book or web page you read. I have tried very hard to ensure that the facts in this book are accurate, but there will be a number of facts where different sources mean discrepancies will occur and opinions will differ.

Also, a very quick note on grammar and structure. Because of the nature of this fact book I have made the conscious decision to use numbers rather than text (for example twelve is written 12). I have done this in an effort to reduce the overall amount of text in the book, which hopefully makes it easier to scan and digest. Apologies in advance to all the grammar purists out there!

With that said, I hope you enjoy reading through some of the facts and that you discover one or two things that you didn't know before.

One last thing, if you are wondering why there are 1,568 facts in this book, make sure you read the first fact in the book!

SMA November 2013

1. GENERAL FACTS

The First World War lasted from 28 July 1914 until 11 November 1918. That is 1,568 days

In total, almost 65 million men were mobilised during the war

The cost of the war is estimated to be $185,000,000,000

Originally, France, Britain and Russia were known as the *Entente Powers*, but as more countries joined in their fight the whole group became to be known as the *Allies*

The *Central Powers* was the term used to describe the wartime alliance of Germany and Austria-Hungary. Later this alliance was extended to include Turkey and Bulgaria

The USA was never officially part of the *Allies*. When they joined the war in 1917, they were officially known as an *Associated Power*

The Western Front was a trench network that covered almost 25,000 miles from the English Channel to the French/Swiss border

The Eastern Front was a huge theatre of war that stretched from the Baltic coast of Latvia to the Black Sea

The Eastern Front was named from a German perspective

The Eastern Front witnesses fighting from three principal empires: Germany, Austria-Hungary and Russia

All of the empires that fought on the Eastern Front were dissolved after the fighting had finished

Fighting on the Eastern Front commenced on 17 August 1914 when the Russian General Pavel Rennenkampf's First Army invaded East Prussia to kick-start the Battle of Tannenberg

On the Eastern Front, the weather played a major part in the way the war was fought. Severe winters and the vast seas of mud created by the spring-time thaw effectively reduced the window of opportunity for launching offensives to a 6 month window between May and October

Twenty-four nations declared war on one or more of the Central Powers throughout the duration of the war

Romania entered the war in August 1916 on the side of the Allies. Just 107 days later armies of the Central Powers entered Bucharest

In those 107 days Romania suffered 305,000 casualties

Before the German army arrived in Bucharest a British sabotage team put out of action $52km^2$ of Romanian oil fields

The first exchange of Prisoners occurred on 15 February 1915 when 10 British and 95 German prisoners were released to go home. Both sets of prisoners travelled through neutral Netherlands

The first air-dropping of supplies onto stricken troops occurred on 27 March 1916 in Mesopotamia. In total, 140 sorties were flown dropping thousands of pounds of flour, sugar, salt and other supplies for the 6th (Poona) Division of the British Indian Army

The first parachute drop of supplies of ammunition occurred on 4 July 1918 on the Western Front near Hamel

The Allied Maritime Transport Council was established in late 1917 to organise the distribution of merchant shipping resources between the Allies for the common good

Brazil declared war on the Central Powers on 26 October 1917

The Brazilian army played no active part in any fighting, however a number of officers were sent to serve with Allied units on the Western Front and a few aircraft mechanics and a number of medical teams also saw active service

One third of the Brazilian officers who served on the Western Front were promoted in the field due to their courage and bravery in battle

It has been estimated that one tonne of explosives fell for every square metre of territory on the Western Front

Wireless telegraphy (W/T) was part of the standard military equipment of all of the major belligerents by 1914 and was widely used by all ground air and sea forces

Allied manpower on the Western Front decreased by around 25% during the end of 1917 and the beginning of 1918, mainly due to the huge number of casualties sustained during large 1917 offensives

During the same period Germany were able to transfer large amounts of men from the East resulting in a 30% increase in manpower by March 1918

2. PRELUDE TO WAR

On 28 June 1914 Archduke Franz Ferdinand, the heir to the throne of the Austro-Hungarian Empire visited the Bosnian capital Sarajevo. He was shot at close range by Gavrilo Princip

Gavrilo Princip was born in Bosnia-Herzegovina in July 1894. He was one of 9 children

Princip used a Browning FN M1910 semi-automatic pistol, serial number 19074, firing a 0.38 ACP round

The terrorist group responsible for the assassination of Franz Ferdinand was called Black Hand, Sarajevo

The Black Hand was a secret society formed in 1911 in an effort to unify all Serbs into one nation

The members of the Black Hand were mainly junior officers of the Serbian national army, but there were also lawyers, academics and journalists in the society

By 1914 there were 2,500 members of the Black Hand

The Black Hand remained active with the Serbian army until December 1916 when the exiled government ordered that the leaders all be arrested

The archduke's assassination by Gavrilo Princip started a domino effect of Allied nation disputes that led to the First World War

Exactly one month after the assassination, on 28 July 1914, Austria declared war on Serbia

On 31 July 1914 in a move in support of Serbia, Russia mobilised its army and moved significant numbers of troops up to the borders of Austria-Hungary and Germany

Germany declared war on Russia on 1 August, citing aggressive Russian behaviour

Kaiser Wilhelm II & the German Government declared war on his cousin, Tsar Nicholas II and Russia

The Schlieffen Plan was the Germany master strategy to win a possible future war on two fronts: against France in the west and Russia in the east

The Schlieffen Plan was devised by Count Alfred von Schlieffen. The first version of the plan was approved in 1899 by Kaiser Wilhelm II

The crux of the Schlieffen Plan was simple: it was thought that Russia would take 6 weeks to mobilise and be ready for war. This gave Germany a theoretical window of 6 weeks to mobilise, beat France and re-organise in order to face Russia

In preparation for the execution of the Schlieffen Plan which involved a general invasion of France, Germany issued an ultimatum to Belgium on 2 August demanding safe passage through her territory. Belgium rejected the ultimatum 24 hours later after securing a pledge of support from Britain in the event of a German invasion

In order to trigger the Schlieffen Plan, Germany declared war on France on 3 August 1914

Seven German Armies were sent forward to invade northern France via Belgium under the terms of the Schlieffen Plan

As part of the Schlieffen Plan, German troops entered Luxembourg on 2 August and moved into Belgium near Liege the next day

As Germany marched through Belgium on the way into France, Britain declared war on Germany on 4 August 1914

3. WEAPONS

Artillery

The Austro-Hungarian Skoda M1911 Howitzer weighed 25,450kg

Big Bertha was the nick-name given to the Krupp 420mm heavy howitzer used by the Germans in WWI. It could fire a 2,050lb (930kg) shell a distance of 9.3 miles (15 km). However, it took a crew of 200 men 6 hours or more to assemble. Germany had 13 of these huge guns

The Big Bertha howitzer was named after the wife of its designer, Gustav Krupp

The Big Bertha howitzer was originally developed for the German army to destroy frontier fortress towns such as Liège as part of the Schlieffen Plan

Over 86 million British 18 pound artillery shells were fired during the war

The 18-pounder shrapnel shell contained 374 small spherical bullets

The 18-pounder shrapnel, if fired at 20 rounds per minute, could deliver 7,480 bullets per minute at a far greater range than machine guns

The French 1897 pattern 75mm field gun was perhaps the most famous gun of the war. Universally known as the Soixainte-Quinze (seventy-five), it was a superb weapon with a fast rate of fire (up to 30 rounds per minute in extreme circumstances) and a range of 9,000 yards

Although excellent in open country, the Soixainte-Quinze was unable to destroy trenches, dugouts and barbed wire entanglements

At the beginning of the war France had no real heavy artillery; the only weapons of this type they could use were 15cm mortars that were relics from the Crimea

It wasn't until April 1915 that the French introduced a 58mm mortar that fired a 20kg bomb over a range of 1,200 yards

A typical field artillery piece required a team of 6: an NCO in command who received and gave orders, a layer who was responsible for the gun's alignment and elevation, a gunner who worked the breech and 3 men for handling the shells and fuses

52% of British artillery shells were fired from 18-pounder field guns

Apart from the very long range guns, artillery targeting was directed by watching where the shells landed and altering gun alignment/elevation accordingly. A forward observation officer (FOO) would relay details back to the gun by telephone or flags

The largest gun of the war was made by German manufacturer Krupp. Nicknamed the 'Paris Gun' it could fire a 210Ib shell over 80 miles

From March to August 1918 the Paris Gun fired over 300 shells on Paris

The Paris Gun was fired from the forest of Courcey, 120km to the north-east of Paris

The first shell landed at 7.18am on 21 March 1918 on the Quai de la Seine. The explosion was heard across the entire city

When the first shells from the Paris Gun landed on Paris, the public thought they were being bombed by a high altitude Zeppelin as neither the sound of a gun nor a plane could be heard

The Paris Gun needed a crew of 80 to work it

In an effort to screen the noise of the gun when it fired, the Paris Gun was surrounded by several field artillery batteries that fired at the same time to stop the gun being spotted by French and British reconnaissance

It took 3 minutes for each shell to travel to its target (Paris)

At the top of its trajectory, the 210Ib shell (94kg) from the Paris Gun climbed to an altitude of 25 miles. At the time it was the highest point ever made by a man-made object

Gunners had to take into consideration the curvature and rotation of the earth when figuring out where the shells from the Paris Gun would land

The Paris Gun killed 250 people, wounded another 620 and caused significant damage to buildings and infrastructure

The Paris Gun was never captured by the Allies. It was returned to Germany in August 1918 where it was destroyed

There were two basic shell types for general field artillery; shrapnel rounds were filled with metal balls and a bursting charge that was set to explode around head-height and high explosive rounds which detonated when the shell hit the ground or a building

Out of the 1,600 artillery pieces involved in the British preliminary bombardment that preceded the Battle of the Somme, 1,200 of them were field guns or medium guns

High explosive artillery shells (HE) were more destructive than shrapnel shells but were very new in 1914 and all sides were struggling to produce reliable HE shells

High explosive artillery shells were designed to explode on impact, however many did not detonate when they landed in the wet mud of Flanders. Both sides developed super-sensitive fuses like the British 106 in order to cope with softer landings in thick mud

By 1916 HE shells dominated artillery bombardments on all sides

When the German army launched their great Spring Offensive (Operation Michael) in 1918 they used 6,473 artillery guns in their opening barrage

In 1915, during the Champagne offensive, France was able to assemble 2,500 artillery guns to support the infantry advance. This number was only achieved by pulling together every available weapon

By 1918 each and every Allied offensive was supported by between 5,000 and 8,000 artillery guns

The gunners of 30th Division, Royal Field Artillery, firing on Bernafay Wood on the Somme, used thermite shells for the first time on 2 July 1916

Thermite shells would deliver balls of molten metal over a wide area upon explosion, causing massive damage to men and machines

One of the many tactical refinements made during the war to the use of artillery in the war was that of the 'creeping barrage'. First instigated during the Battle of the Somme in August 1916, British artillery fire moved forward in stages just in front of the advancing infantry

By the autumn of 1916 the British had perfected the art of a creeping barrage advancing at 50 metres per minute

Most anti-aircraft commanders initially preferred to fire shrapnel rounds for ground to air shooting. By 1918 incendiary rounds which threw out balls of flaming thermite were becoming more common

Barbed Wire

In order to deploy or fix barbed wire in No Man's Land wiring parties were sent out under cover of darkness. It was one of the most dangerous tasks in the front line

Wiring posts were approximately 6ft high, originally British wiring parties would hammer these posts into the ground with a muffled mallet. However the noise would often alert the enemy and as a consequence many men on duty with wiring parties were either killed or wounded

Eventually the British redesigned their wire posts to be screwed into the ground which was almost silent

Where the distance between the enemy front lines was short wiring parties would often encounter men from the opposing line doing exactly the same task. In this situation hand-to-hand fighting would occur – the sound of which would alert machine-gunners on both sides who would strafe No Man's Land

Trench Weapons

Early war hand grenades were prone to explode prematurely, making them very dangerous

One of the most common and effective hand grenades of the war was the British Mills Bomb (officially known as the No.5 grenade)

The most iconic grenade of the war was the German 'potato masher' stick grenade (Stielhandgranate)

On the night of 26 July 1916 at Poziers, British and Australian troops exchanged grenade fire with the enemy continuously for over 12 hours – throwing over 15,000 hand grenades

As with most grenades, the Mills Bomb had a lethal radius that was greater than the distance it could be thrown, so the thrower had to be able to run for cover once he had let go

Trench systems provided perfect hand grenade cover and as such these weapons proved very effective in trench raids

The British army eventually developed their own specialist grenade teams or 'bombing parties'. These teams were made up of 9 men; 2 designated throwers, 2 carriers, 2 bayonet men and 2 spares to take over in the case of any member of the team being wounded

Mortars are short range weapons that fire shells at a high trajectory. They were perfect mobile weapons to fire from trench to trench

All Allied trench mortars were smooth bored, whereas German trench mortars were rifle bored in a bid to aid accuracy

One of the best mortars on either side was the British Stokes Mortar, named after its creator, Sir Wilfred Stokes; they began to be used from 1916

The British Stoke Mortar was truly portable as it could be broken down into parts. It needed a crew of 2 to operate and could fire 22, 3 inch rounds per minute

'Minnie' was a term used to describe the German trench mortar minnenwerfer (another such term was Moaning Minnie)

At the outbreak of war, Britain had absolutely no trench mortars whatsoever

The 240mm French Batignolles trench mortar fired a 192Ib bomb that could left a crater 30 feet across and 10 feet deep

Britain was so slow to equip front line troops with adequate numbers of grenades that soldiers were forced to improvise and build their own using tins, glass jars and bits of scrap metal

An alternative to the hand grenade was the rifle grenade. Although these could cover greater distances, accuracy of fire was often poor

William Mills, a hand grenade designer from Sunderland, patented, developed and manufactured the 'Mills Bomb' at the Mills munitions factory in Birmingham in 1915

Approximately 75,000,000 British No.5 grenades were made during the war

The German army used 270 million grenades of all types on all fronts during the war

A small number of 'special' grenades were manufactured by the French and appeared in 1916. Designed for effectively clearing trenches and deep dug outs, these 'specials' contained either tear gas, phosphorous or calorite which was a compound that burned at temperatures touching 3,000 degrees

Flamethrowers

Germans were the first to use flamethrowers (flammenwerfer) in WWI. Their flamethrowers could fire jets of flame as far as 130 feet (40 m)

During the war it is estimated that Germany launched over 650 separate flame thrower attacks

There were two types of German flamethrowers: The Kleif (Kleinflammenwefer or small flamethrower) and the Wex

The Kleif was not really small and needed a crew of 2 to work it; one to carry the fuel container on his back and the other who aimed and fired the weapon. It had a range of 25m

The Wex was a one-man weapon with the fuel carried on the

soldiers' back in a special container. It had a range of 20m

Because of the highly combustible nature of the flammenwerfers and the short range these weapons had to operate at to be effective the men who worked these weapons were often targeted by concentrated small arms fire. It was a very dangerous job

The French developed their own flamethrower called the Schilt (named after his creator). It carried more fuel than the German designs and had a range of 30m

During the 1916 Somme offensive, the British built 4 large flamethrowers into strong points 60 metres from the German line. Each flamethrower weighed 2 tonnes

Tanks and Armoured Cars

British tanks were initially called landships. However, in an attempt to disguise them as water storage tanks rather than as weapons, the British decided to code name them 'tanks'

'Little Willie' was the first prototype tank in WWI. Built in 1915, it carried a crew of 3 and could travel as fast as 3 mph (4.8 km/h)

The name 'Little Willie' is said to be an uncomplimentary dig at the then
German Crown Prince

The first 50 tanks arrived in France on 30 August 1916 and were added to the Machine Gun Corps

During WWI, British tanks were initially categorized into 'males' and 'females'. Male tanks had cannons, while females had heavy machine guns

The only tank built and produced for the Germany army was the A7V Panzerkampfwagen. Only 20 saw active service during the war

The A7V was the heaviest (32 tons) and the best armoured (30mm thick) tank produced on either side during the war

In early British tanks the engine was in the same place where the crew worked. As well as being full of poisonous petrol and exhaust fumes, temperatures inside reached 50° C

With poor ventilation, British tank crews were often poisoned by engine and gun fumes

The first ever combat tank was the British MKI. It was first used in action during the morning of 15 September 1916 during the Battle of Flers-Courcellete

Throughout the course of the war 8,237 tanks were produced on all sides

Early tanks had no wireless radio; communication with command posts was made by pigeon

The French built Renault FT tank was the first tank to have its main gun housed within a turret that could rotate 360 degrees

The top speed of the British MKI tank was 4.5km/h

Early British tanks were built in either 'male' or 'female' formats. The males carried two 6 pounder guns and 3 machine guns, whereas the female version had 5 machine guns

The first armoured cars were nothing more than civilian motors with armour plating bolted to the sides and the roof

In the UK, Rolls Royce, Lanchester and Wolseley were the main producers of armoured cars, with Daimler and Ehrhardt manufacturing similar cars in Germany, Peugeot and Renault working in France and Fiat and Lancia in Italy

Early uses of armoured cars were for intelligence gathering, counter-attacking at speed and pursuing a retreating enemy

Armoured cars were most effective in mobile operations over flat ground; as a consequence trench warfare on the Western Front meant they were rarely used effectively in the front line after the initial skirmishes of 1914 until late in 1918 when a mobile war re-emerged

The armour on armoured cars was only very light and although might have been reasonably effective against rifle fire, it stood no chance against artillery

Gas

The French were the first to use gas in combat, using tear gas grenades against the Germans in August 1914

On 22 April 1915 Germany used clouds of chlorine gas for the first time as part of an infantry advance. The results were good. The assaulting troops advanced more than a mile within an hour, with hardly a shot fired

The special engineers who managed the poison gas for the German army were called 'Stinkpionere'

Gas was released in 2 different ways. Either by large canisters that released large quantities of gas vapour in the general direction of the enemy (this was wholly dependent on wind and weather conditions). Alternatively artillery shells were filled with liquid gas that evaporated when the shell burst

During WWI the Germans released about 68,000 tons of gas. The British and French released about 51,000 tons each. In total, 1,200,000 soldiers on both sides were gassed, of which 91,198 died horrible deaths

Approximately 30 different poisonous gases were used during WWI

Before gas masks were issued to front line troops, soldiers were told to hold a urine-soaked cloth over their faces in a gas emergency

The first gas masks were nothing more than a pair of goggles and a piece of chemical soaked cloth, but as war progressed gas protection became more sophisticated, culminating in full face mask and respirator

By 1918, gas masks with filter respirators usually provided effective protection. At the end of the war, many countries signed treaties outlawing chemical weapons

Rifles, Bayonets and Pistols

The British army used the Short Magazine Lee Enfield (SMLE) rifle as their rifle of choice

British officers and men were instructed to clean their weapons every day to ensure they were always working at their optimum

In the British army, a dirty weapon was a military crime that could be punishable by loss of pay or, worse case, a court martial.

Most rifles on all sides had similar performance. Maximum range was around 3,500 yards, however most armies did not expect any individual to hit a specific target beyond 600 yards

In the trenches, British troops kept their rifle sights set at 200 yards at all times to enable them to fire accurately into No Man's Land

'Rapid fire' for the average soldier under battle conditions was typically around 8-12 rounds per minute

Germany produced a bayonet with a saw blade, featuring a double row of teeth. Although only initially produced for special engineering groups that required a saw, it added to the vision that the Germans were ruthless, bloodthirsty 'Huns'.

The main infantry weapon of the German army was the 1898 7.9mm

Mauser rifle

German officers, NCOs, machine-gunners and some storm troops carried the 1908 9mm Luger, although Mausers were also carried

Highly trained regulars from the British Expeditionary Force were able to achieve 15-20 rounds per minute

Any individual that excelled in the art of rifle fire was earmarked for a special role as a sniper

Snipers often operated in remote, heavily camouflaged positions. They usually worked with a spotter who used binoculars or a trench periscope to identify potential targets

As well as a rifle, all infantrymen were issued with a bayonet; a blade that attached to the barrel of their rifle for use in times of close combat

There were 3 types of bayonet; the most common were shaped like a blade of a knife, whilst others were much thinner 'needle' types. Some specialist German troops were issued with bayonets with serrated blades

In reality, bayonet charges were very rare. In most cases the bayonet was more often employed in opening food tins, scraping mud from boots, toasting bread and other more mundane purposes

German infantry had 2 main types of rifle; the Mauser Gewehr 88 and the Mauser Gewehr 98 – first made in 1888 and 1898 respectively. The Mauser 98 was exceptionally accurate and continued in service into WW2

The Mauser Automatic was probably the most powerful pistol in operation during the war. It had a muzzle velocity of 440m/second

The basic infantry weapon of the French infantry was the 8mm Lebel rifle. The Lebel was originally designed in 1886 and updated in 1896

The 8mm Lebel was not a great rifle due to slow re-load times and was replaced in 1905 with the 1907 Berthier

It took some time to replace the Lebel rifle completely, but by 1917 all new recruits were issued with the Berthier

Lebel rifles continued to see use at the front as rifle grenades; some were also preferred by snipers

Accompanying French rifles was the 1886 pattern bayonet, which was long at 45cm and quite slender. It had a tendency to snap.

The bayonet charge was something of legend in France. The charge, with bugles sounding and colours flying was something of wonder to many. The bayonet was even given a nickname 'Rosalie'

Gavrilo Princip used a Belgian made 7.6mm Browning Model 1900 to assassinate Archduke Franz Ferdinand on 28 June 1914

Pistols were used mainly by the officer class and specialist troops such as the Tank Corps, miners, military police and pilots.

Many officers swapped their pistol for a rifle during offensives in an effort to blend in with the massed ranks of the infantry

British revolver manufacturer Webley produced more than 300,000 guns for the war effort, but even this wasn't enough to meet demand. Many officers and men of the Royal Navy or RFC/RAF could be seen sporting US Colt automatics

Some US infantry carried the Model 12 Winchester shotgun. A 12 gauge pump action weapon it was capable of scattering large amounts of 0.32 calibre pellets over a wide range. It was a very effective 'trench broom'

The Winchester shotgun was equipped with a lug attachment to take the 1917 Enfield bayonet

The main drawback to the Winchester shotgun was the shells that were made of cardboard and thus susceptible to damp and the rain. In the muddy and wet conditions of the Western Front they were largely useless

Before the development of specific anti-aircraft weaponry, ground forces would fire rifles and machine guns at hostile aircraft

The principal Italian rifle was the 6.5mm bolt action Mannlicher-Carcano M1891 which boasted a 6 shot magazine

Machine Guns

During the attack at High Wood on 24 August 1916 it is estimated that ten British Vickers machine guns fired over one million rounds in 12 hours

In 1914 the German army deployed an average of 24 machine-guns per division. By early 1918 this had grown to 358

During 1916 the number of machine guns in service within the German army doubled from 8,000 to 16,000

In 1914 the German High Command calculated that the fire power of one heavy machine-gun was equal to that of 80 riflemen

Machine-guns of the war boasted impressive fire power – 600 rounds per minute was common, although firing at that speed caused the barrel to overheat quickly

There were 2 ways of cooling the barrel; air-cooled (using radiating fins attached to the barrel) or water, where the barrel was wrapped in a water jacket

Most machine-guns weighed between 30-40kg with some of the heavy machine-guns over 50kg. These weights do not include ammunition

A British Vickers heavy machine-gun was often accompanied by at least a dozen 250-round ammunition belts, each weighing 10kg

The average machine-gun needed two or three men to fire it, but often had a team of up to six men to manage it properly

Eventually lighter machine-gun models were introduced on all sides, which enabled the weapon and its team to keep up with attacking infantry. These generally weighed 10-14kg and could fire 250-600 rounds per minute

The first machine-gun introduced into the French army was the 1897 Hotchkiss

The Hotchkiss was fed by aluminium trays each holding 24 rounds each, instead of belts of ammunition like other machine-guns

Another difference between the Hotchkiss and other machine guns was the fact the Hotchkiss was air-cooled and therefore didn't need water blankets to cool the barrel as it fired

During the battle of Verdun, one section of 2 Hotchkiss machine guns was isolated by advancing German troops but managed to hold off the enemy for ten days and nights. During this time the 2 guns are thought to have fired over 75,000 rounds

The German Maschinengewehr 08 was the defacto heavy machine-gun for the German army. It is estimated that this gun accounted for 90% of all British casualties on the first day of the Battle of the Somme

The water blanket of the German Maxim heavy machine-gun held 7.5 pints of water which reached boiling point after 1 minute of continuous firing

By the beginning of 1916 the German army possessed over 8,000 machine guns. By July 1916, this had increased to nearer 11,000 and by the end of the year there were 16,000 machine guns in action

The world's first sub-machine-gun was the 9mm Bergmann Maschinenpistole 18/1 which was light enough for use by assault troops. It was introduced in early 1918 but was not present in significant numbers until the middle of 1918 when Germany was not really capable of any more major offensives

The 9mm Bergmann worried the Allies so much that they wrote a clause in the Treaty of Versailles forbidding the manufacture of this weapon

The Italian army entered the war with only 600 working machine guns, but by the time of the Armistice it had over 12,000

The main machine gun of choice for the Italian army was the Fiat-Revelli M1914 which was tripod mounted and used a 50 round cartridge. The Italian army also used small numbers of Maxim and Hotchkiss machine-guns too

Mines

The first underground explosions (mines) of the war were detonated by Germany on 20 December 1914 underneath a brigade of Indian troops near Festubert

The first British mines were detonated at Hill 60 on the Ypres salient on 17 April 1915 and used 10,000lb of explosives

The opening salvos of the Battle of the Somme in July 1916 were preceded by the blowing of 17 separate mines, the largest of which used 54,000Ib of ammonal, threw debris 1,200m feet in the air and produced a crater that was almost 100m across and 30m deep

Artillery barrages and mines created immense noise. In 1917, explosives blowing up beneath the German lines on Messines Ridge at Ypres in Belgium could be heard in London 140 miles (220km) away

There were over 8000m of tunnels dug under the Messines Ridge by the summer of 1917. Within those tunnels, twenty-one separate mines were laid that together held over 400 tonnes of ammonal

The mines under Messines Ridge were detonated at 3.10am on 7 June 1917. The eruption was so large it destroyed an estimated 10,000 German soldiers instantly and it was clearly heard in London and southern England

The largest crater made by the Messines Ridge explosion was formed by a single mine of 91,000lb of ammonal. The crater, called Lone Tree was 12m deep and 76m across

Lone Tree was purchased by Lord Wakefield after the war and transformed into the 'Pool of Peace', which is now a memorial

There is still one unexploded mine shaft under the Messines Ridge

At the height of the mining activity underneath the Messines Ridge there were about 20,000 British Canadian, Australian and New Zealand tunnellers employed in digging deadly holes in the ridge, and about as many Germans digging straight towards them

4. TRENCH WARFARE

Between September and November 1914 each side tried to outflank each other in a series of small skirmishes which naturally extended both lines further north until they literally ran out land. This 'race to the sea' ended in two continuous lines of trenches running from the Franco-Swiss border right up to the north Belgium coast

Early wartime trenches were little more than connected foxholes and were not designed for long term use

On the Western Front the trenches ran through towns and villages, through industrial works, across railway tracks, through farms, fields and woods, across rivers, canals and streams. Each feature presented its own set of challenges for the men who had to dig in and defend

The open space between two sets of opposing trenches became known as No Man's Land. It was such a dangerous place to be no soldier wanted to be out there

Most commonly associated with the First World War the phrase No Man's Land actually dates back until at least the 14th century

The average distance of No Man's Land between two sets of opposing trenches was about 250 yards

The narrowest gap of No Man's Land was at Zonnebeke where British and German soldiers were sometimes no more than 7 yards apart

New troops to the front line had a natural inclination to peer over the parapet to see No Man's Land, despite being warned not to do so. Many men died on their first day in the trenches as a consequence of a well-aimed sniper bullet

Trenches in the vicinity of the River Somme were dug into ground that was very chalky. The trenches were relatively easy to dig initially but were liable to crumble after rain and needed a lot of maintenance. The walls of the trenches were 'revetted' (reinforced) with wood or sandbags to minimise the crumbling effects

Around Ypres, in the Flanders region of Belgium, the ground is naturally very wet and as a consequence trenches were not really dug too far into the ground but built up with wood and sandbags. These were called breastworks

Breastworks were often 7 or 8 foot high. In some places they were 30 foot high

The conditions of trenches varied greatly depending on the local conditions
All trenches were usually built in a zig-zag with angular 'fire-bays' to minimise the effect of shell fire and to prevent the enemy from firing down the length of the trench

Dugouts were protective holes cut deep underground to offer front line troops a bit more protection from enemy shellfire

In breastworks, dugouts were made by leaving space for a shelter then having it roofed

A manual published by the British army recommended dugouts to be between 2 feet and 4 feet 6 inches wide, roofed with corrugated iron or brushwood then covered with a minimum of 9 inches of earth

Dugouts at Messines in 1917 were huge and could hold an entire Battalion of men

Deep dugouts would be up to 10 feet underground and used by senior officers for meetings as well as rest and protection from artillery bombardment

Deep dugouts were entered via a stairway, the entrance of which would often be covered by a gas proof curtain to protect the inhabitants from any gas attack
This gas curtain would act as a killer too. If a soldier entered the dugout after a gas attack he could bring gas in on his boots and clothing which would not be able to escape due to the curtain. It was not unheard of for members of a dugout to be gassed and killed whilst sleeping in this way

Such deep dugouts often had two or more rooms and were equipped with electricity for lighting as well as beds and other pieces of furniture

German trenches were generally better built and maintained than the Allied lines, mainly because the Allies were always looking to be on the attack and didn't think they would be in their own trenches for long

The German army pioneered the use of second line trenches from autumn 1915 and also introduced concrete strong points and a third line of trenches
The typical type of system consisted of 3 lines of trenches about 800 yards apart and connected by communications trenches

The first line of trenches, the one nearest the enemy, was called the fire trench. The second line of trench was called the support trench and the third line of trench was called the reserve trench

Communication trenches were dug at an angle to those facing the enemy and were used to transport men equipment and rations

A 'listening post' was an advanced post or 'sap', usually in No Man's

Land, where soldiers tried to find out information about the enemy

Saps were narrow, shallow trenches about 30 yards long dug at right angles to the front line trench extending right out in to No Man's Land towards the enemy

There were millions of rats in WW1 trenches. A pair of rodents could produce as many as 900 young a year in trench conditions so soldiers' attempts to kill them were futile

There were two main types of rat; the brown and the black rat. Both were despised but the brown rat was especially feared. Gorging themselves on human remains (grotesquely disfiguring them by eating their eyes and liver), they could grow to the size of a cat

Men would attempt kill the rats using various methods including shooting them, stabbing them with a bayonet and even by clubbing them to death

As well as rats, lice were another problem. They bred in the seams of filthy clothing and as well as causing the men to itch constantly, they caused 'Trench Fever' – a particularly painful episode that included high fever and intense pain. Recovery could take up to 12 weeks

Lice were not actually identified as the cause of 'Trench Fever' until 1918
The French tended to use tramways in their communication trenches, whereas the British soldiers carried supplies right to the front line in 'carrying parties'

These carrying parties took supplies of water, rations, ammunition, bombs, wire and other equipment up to the front line

Communication trenches were also used to carry wounded soldiers out of the front line towards casualty clearing stations

In some areas, communication trenches were traversed like the front line trenches and had fire steps built in, just in case the enemy broke through

A typical pattern of routine would be 4 days in the front line, 4 days in the second line, 4 days in reserve and then 4 days rest. Although this varied enormously based on conditions, weather and resources

It was not unusual for the length of time in the front line trenches to be much longer and 30 day stints were common

On one occasion the 13th Yorkshire and Lancashire Regiment spent 51 consecutive days in the front line

The relief of a unit in the front line trench was a time of tension and danger. The noise and movement of so many men moving in and out of a relatively small area increased the risk of attracting enemy attention. A couple of well-placed artillery shells could be devastating

Infantry units were almost always swapped in and out of the front line under cover of darkness

During the night, perhaps 1 man in 4 was posted on sentry duty, often positioned in saps dug a little way in advance of the main front line trench. Their job was to listen and watch for signs of enemy activity

Night sentry duty would last for one hour; each man on duty would stand on the fire-step with their head and shoulders above the parapet

During this time, men on sentry duty were not allowed to wear anything that would cover their ears. In the winter this would be very uncomfortable due to the cold and wind

Whilst working as a sentry, falling asleep on duty or failing to observe or report enemy activity was a crime that would result in a court-martial and could be punishable by death

Although the threat of a death sentence hung over the men on sentry duty only 2 British men were executed for this crime during the war

To stop themselves from falling asleep some soldiers rested their chins on the tip of their bayonet

During the day, sentry duty was reduced to perhaps one man in ten

During dawn and dusk, the entire front line on all sides was ordered to 'Stand To!' Every man was put on full alert in case of enemy attack

Along most of the Western Front, the Allied troops were looking directly into the sunrise during the morning 'Stand To!' This made observation of No Man's Land very difficult and made the watching Allied troops more susceptible to enemy snipers

Accompanying 'Stand To!' in the morning was another daily ritual nicknamed 'morning hate'. Both sides would let off machine-gun, artillery and small arms fire into the mist of No Man's Land to make doubly sure no enemy was about to attack

In almost every part of the line both sides tried to observe an unofficial truce for part of the morning to allow breakfast to be served

Approximately 30 minutes before sunset the front line trench was again ordered to 'Stand To!' This state of alert would continue to full darkness and the threat of an enemy raid in the receding light had passed

During the evening 'Stand To!' all men were ordered to stand on the trench floor with their bayonets 'fixed'. As darkness set in, the men moved up to the fire step, crouching below the parapet until full darkness when it was safe to stand fully upright with head and shoulders above the trench line

During 'Stand To!' no one could talk, smoke or move around

British NCOs had to inspect the men's rifles twice a day and ensure all fighting equipment and ammunition were all present and correct

In order to raise the alert of a gas attack many British trenches had an empty shell casing hung by a wire that would be hit like a gong with a bit of wood

Rations and supplies needed by the front line trenches were brought up to the line during the hours of darkness. The enemy knew this and often shelled known supply routes

The front of the trench was known as the 'parapet' with the rear of the trench known as the 'parados'

Both parapet and parados were protected by 2 or 3 feet of sandbags

Soldiers were instructed to build the parados higher than the parapet so that defenders were not outlined in the sky and therefore easy targets for enemy snipers

The parados was built up with sandbags as protection from 'friendly' artillery fire as well as protection from the enemy if they broke through the lines and attacked from the rear

It has been estimated that about 75,000 British soldiers were killed during the war by 'friendly' artillery fire intended for the enemy

Sandbags were filled with earth by dedicated filling parties

A filling party consisted of one soldier filling the bags with a shovel and two other men holding and tying the bags

Other men, working in pairs, would move and stack the filled sandbags. A pair of men could be expected to move 60 bags in an hour

It was suggested by British army research that a typical bullet would only penetrate 15cm into a sandbag

To enable soldiers to fire through gaps in the sandbags on the parapet a fire step was dug into the wall of the trench. It was on this firestep that sentries stood

German defences became more complex in 1916 when they adopted a 'defence in depth' strategy towards trench warfare. With this setup the line nearest the enemy was only lightly held, it was not designed to stop the attackers, but to delay them or channel them into more exposed 'Killing Zones'. Perhaps 1 mile beyond this was another line of strong points that were well within the range of the defending artillery. The point of this line was to funnel attacking troops once more into the 'Battle Zone' which was typically an area about a mile wide which was full of strong points and multi-level trenches, all of which were capable of 360 degree fire. The reserve zone even further behind held yet more defence systems

By late 1916 the British and French armies were also on adopting the 'defence in depth' strategy

'Defence in depth' often resulted in many more casualties from both sides. Intense fighting took place in small confined 'battle zones' which were constantly shelled by both sides

The most formidable example of 'defence in depth' was the German Hindenburg Line which was situated in the central and northern reaches of the Western Front

The Germans started constructing the Hindenburg Line in September 1916 and it was still being built in late 1918

The term 'line' in regards to the Hindenburg Line is a misnomer as it was actually a series of strongholds and fortifications that were linked together with trenches

Each individual strongpoint had its own system of secondary supporting fortifications, covered with barbed wire, trenches and machine-guns

In many places the Hindenburg Line was 15km deep

Trench raids, which were local night attacks aimed at capturing prisoners, gathering intelligence and generally causing a nuisance to the enemy, were first initiated by the British in November 1914

By 1916, the trench raid was practically a daily occurrence up and down all front lines

To stop British night patrols the Germans used a light shell rocket. It was a flare that was fired into the sky and used a parachute to keep it in the air for over a minute. Blazing brightly it gave the defending troops a chance to spot and fire upon any enemy soldiers who had advanced into No Man's Land

140,000 Chinese labourers served on the Western Front over the course of the First World War. Their main task was to dig trenches

Supply of trenches on the Western Front was maintained by huge amounts of lorries and horse drawn wagons and the proliferation of railway spurs on both sides of the front line

Supply of front line troops was a perennial problem for all armies. Light railways were used for a large proportion of supplies but these were easy targets for enemy guns. Motor transport was harder to disrupt and used more and more as the war progressed, although trucks and other motor transport struggled to move across smashed roads and muddy fields

Maintenance and logistics such as construction of trenches and repairing the lines, laying cables and fixing barbed wire were mostly carried out at night

Communication was very unreliable and hinged on huge field telephone networks. Phone wires were often broken by enemy shell fire and human and animal messengers were always required as a back up

German trenches were in stark contrast to British trenches. German trenches were built to last and included bunk beds, furniture, cupboards, water tanks with faucets, electric lights, and doorbells

Christmas 1914 saw a spontaneous truce in many parts of the Western Front where opposing soldiers met in No Man's Land where they swapped photos, badges, and cigarettes. In some places they played football

Saps were short lengths of trenches that were dug out into No Man's Land in an effort to get closer to enemy trenches with limited exposure to enemy fire

If a line was drawn through the German defensive lines at any point on the Somme that line would cross through 13 separate trenches

The accumulation of water in the bottom of the trenches caused many soldiers' feet to be badly infected, an infliction known as 'trench foot'

'Trench foot' was a fungal infection of the feet caused by cold, wet and unsanitary trench conditions. It could turn gangrenous and result in amputation

In an effort to reduce the effects of 'trench foot' wooden planking, known as duckboards, were placed at the bottom of the trenches and across other muddy areas

Self inflicted harm was common in the trenches as soldiers became desperate to get a 'Blighty wound' that would result in them being sent to a hospital in England to recover. The most common method was to shoot themselves in the foot

The front line trenches generally stank badly from a number of nasty sources: rotting bodies lay around in their thousands, poison gas, rotting sandbags, cigarette smoke, cordite, overflowing latrines, thousands of men that hadn't had a bath in weeks and chloride of lime which was liberally applied all over the trenches to try and limit the spread of disease

In British trenches the word given to trench toilets was 'latrine'

Latrines were usually nothing more than pits 4 foot deep that were dug at the end of a short sap or a bay off of a communication trench

A soldier had to ask permission to leave the front line trench and he had to take his rifle and all kit with him

Each company had two sanitary personnel whose job it was to keep the latrines in as good as condition as possible

In many units, officers gave out latrine duties as punishment

Before a change of regiments in the trenches, the outgoing unit was supposed to fill in their latrines and dig new ones for the newly arriving men

Toilet paper was not issued and soldiers had to improvise with whatever they could lay their hands on

Funk holes were small areas scraped out of the side of the trench where the men would rest and try and catch some sleep, although many officers thought funk holes were too dangerous and banned men from sleeping in them in their trenches

When it rained, soldiers would drape waterproof sheets across funk holes in an effort to keep dry

After heavy bombardments soldiers were ordered to go out and seize any new craters in No Man's Land which could then be used as listening posts

From August 1916 the British Army were under orders to occupy any shell hole within 60 yards of their own trench

Almost all trenches on both sides were protected by thick belts of barbed wire entanglements

Barbed wire was usually placed far enough from the trenches to prevent the enemy from getting close enough to throw grenades

In some areas the belts of barbed wire were up to 100 yards (30 metres) thick

Sometimes gaps in the barbed wire were left on purpose to channel attacking infantry into zones that were covered by machine guns and artillery

Barbed wire entanglements were virtually impossible to pass through. Before major attacks groups of soldiers were sent into No Man's Land   with wire cutters to cut a path through the enemy wire

Another way to attempt to clear enemy wire was to place a bangalore torpedo (a long pipe filled with explosive) under the wire and detonate it

Despite the cold and the general conditions in the trenches each British soldier was expected to wash and shave every day. The reason for this was three-fold; to instil a sense of discipline in the men, to maintain cleanliness as much as possible to stop the spread of disease and to ensure their respirators fitted against their faces properly (they didn't seal fully unless clean-shaven)

Life in the trenches was heavily regulated and run by time-tables which required accurate time keeping. Because watches of that era could easily lose or gain time, regular 'synchronisation' of watches was needed to ensure everyone was working to the same time

A 'jumping off trench' was a shallow and quickly dug trench or ditch, positioned a few yards in front of the front line trench and was intended to gain the attackers a few yards of ground before an advance or attack

No Man's Land was often lit up with bright flares, star shells and coloured rockets that were all fired into the sky during the night

'Very lights' were fired by special pistols held by officers – the bright light balls would make it easy to spot enemy working parties or raiding parties that were out in No Man's Land

'Very lights' were named after their inventor; the American Edward W Very

'Pill Box' was the term given to concrete fortifications that were built in an effort to strengthen defensive positions. They often housed machine-gun crews

In the trenches in the Vosges area of the front winter temperatures dropped so low that bread and wine froze

Machine-gunners saw themselves as above the average infantry man. They were often excused sentry duty and so often benefited from a good night's sleep, they also had to be continuously next to their weapon, so were also exempt from carrying and working parties. Such privileges did not endear them to their infantry counterparts

.

5. THE WAR IN THE AIR

General

There were approximately 70 different types of planes in WW1

On 1 August 1915, two German pilots became the first to shoot down another aircraft using a forward facing machine gun

The term 'dogfight' was originally used my members of the Royal Flying Corps to describe aerial combat. It was taken from the Victorian slang term for a 'riotous brawl'

The first dogfight is generally considered to have taken place over Flanders on 26 April 1917 and involved 94 aircraft

The Allies lost 2.2 planes for every one lost by Germany and the Central Powers

During April 1917, the British lost 245 aircraft, 211 aircrew killed or missing and 108 as prisoners of war – it was dubbed 'Bloody April'

In contrast, Germany lost just 66 machines during the same month

The war in the air was much more prevalent on the Western Front than on the Eastern Front

When they entered the war, Italy boasted just 58 front line ready aircraft

More than half of Manfred von Richthofen's 80 kills were of reconnaissance aircraft

Reconnaissance aircraft were deemed so important that fighter aircraft were designed specifically to shoot them down or to protect them from enemy fighters

In March 1915 a French pilot, Roland Garros fitted steel plates to the propeller of his plane so that bullets from a forward facing machine gun would not damage his propeller. This 'deflector gear' gave the Allies an advantage in aerial battles for a short time

In April 1915 Germany captured an Allied machine with 'deflector gear' fitted and worked on building a better version

Soon afterwards, Fokker, the Dutch plane manufacturer, came up with the 'interrupter gear' which prevented a machine-gun from firing when a propeller blade passed in front of the gun barrel. This invention transformed aerial combat

300 Fokker E-1 monoplanes fitted with the interrupter gear shot down over a thousand Allied machines in what became known as the 'Fokker Scourge'

It took the Allies until the spring of 1916 to gain some sort of parity once more in the battle for the skies

The pilots of the US Army Air Service went into combat flying British and French planes

The typical fighter plane equipped with machine guns were only able to enjoy 50 seconds of fire

At the beginning of the war Russia possessed over 350 machines, more than many other warring nations, but many were obsolete and not fit for service

As well as these planes, the Russians also possessed 16 airships in 1914

By 1917 there were more than 1,000 Russian planes in service over the Eastern Front but they failed to make any real impact

The Ansaldo A-1 was the first Italian designed fighter plane to enter war service. Developed in 1917 it was known as the 'Balilla' (Hunter). Around 150 were built

In August 1914 the Belgian *Compagnie des Aviateurs* boasted a single squadron equipped with a dozen machines

A professional *Aviation Militaire* was developed in early 1915 to support Belgian troops on the Western Front. It consisted of 5 working squadrons

By the end of the war the Belgian *Aviation Militaire* had grown to 11 squadrons operating some 140 frontline machines

In the run up to the war Russia had just one aviation company for each Army Corps. A total of 224 aircraft were available

By the Autumn of 1914 the Russian Air Service had lost around 140 machines

The air war over the Eastern Front was very active, but it was much more one-sided than that on the Western Front. The Central Powers had almost total dominance

Russia struggled to manufacture and repair their aircraft quickly enough to keep enough machines in the air and was forced to import planes to help the cause

Between 1915 and the end of 1917 Russia imported around 1,800 aircraft and 4,000 engines, mostly from France, in an effort to ease the burden on the Russian manufacturing system

On 9 December 1917 the Russian Air Service had 579 serviceable aircraft

The US Air Corps of 1917 consisted of 55 antiquated machines and 26 qualified pilots, some of whom had been trained by the Wright Brothers

American pilots were trained both in American and in Europe, with final battle training taking place in France

It is estimated that during the training period one pilot was killed for every 18 who successfully graduated

Individual American pilots flew with Allied squadrons until April 1918 when their own US squadrons became operational

It is estimated that US pilots accounted for 781 enemy planes and 73 enemy balloons sert chapter five text here. Insert chapter five text here.

Strategic Bombing

Following a French air raid on Freiburg, the Kaiser gave approval for the aerial bombing of Britain on 10 January 1915 although he stressed that damage to royal properties and historical buildings was forbidden

There were a total of 675 Allied air raids over Germany

Germany had planned strategic bombing raids using planes over England from the beginning of the war. They raised a specialist squadron for this specific task and in an effort to disguise its mission it was called the Ostend Carrier Pigeon Squadron

The first specialist long range bomber built by Germany was the Gotha bomber. The G IV were 40 foot long, had a wingspan of 78 foot and with a powerful Mercedes engine could fly at 15,000 foot fully loaded at 80mph

The Gotha had a crew of 3, boasted 3 machine guns and could carry over 250g of bombs

Gothas were very unstable on landing and more Gothas were lost due to crash landings than were lost in action

In September 1917 Germany introduced a new version of the strategic bomber. The Staaken Riesen type bombers were more than double the size of Gothas and were aptly nicknamed 'Giants'

Staaken Giants could carry 2 tons of bombs over 300 miles

Britain manufactured her own heavy bomber; the Handley Page V/1500 was nicknamed the 'Bloody Paralyser'

The Handley Page V/1500 was built to enable the direct bombing of Berlin from the east of England

Only 3 'Bloody Paralysers' were operational by the Armistice

The first air raid over Britain occurred on 21 December 1914 when a Friedchshafen FF29 seaplane took off from Belgium with the south-east as its target. It dropped 2 small bombs; however they both fell into the sea near Dover

Three days later, on Christmas Eve, the first German bomb landed on English soil when another Friedchshafen FF29 seaplane followed the same route to Kent and dropped a bomb close to Dover castle. Damage was limited to a few broken windows

The RFC/RAF dropped 660 tonnes of bombs over German strategic targets during the war. Twice as much as Germany did on Allied targets

Zeppelins and Airships

The first rigid airship was demonstrated by Count Ferdinand von Zeppelin on 2 July 1900 at Friedrichshafen, Southern Germany

The first airship was 420 foot long and was named LZ1 (Luftschiff Zeppelin 1).

After numerous improvements and changes, LZ3 was finalised in 1907 and was capable of 8 hours continuous flight. As a result it could travel further and longer than any plane and could carry passengers and a load. The German army was impressed and ordered one – (LZ4)

LZ4 was destroyed in a storm before the army could get any use out of it. It could have spelt the end of the airship programme but the German public donated enough money to enable more development

Germany built 2 airship variants; the well-known Zeppelin and the less well known Schütte-Lanz. Both were kept in the skies by hydrogen gas

Early Zeppelins were around 158 metres long, could travel at 45mph and carried a crew of 16 men

The first German airship raid on England was on 19 January 1915. Zeppelins L3 and L4 dropped a number of high explosive and incendiary bombs over Norfolk, killing 4 and injuring 16

The temperature in the gondolas of Zeppelins would often fall to -25°C and below

In an effort to combat altitude sickness due to the thin air, the Zeppelin crew carried bottles of liquid oxygen and mouthpieces to breathe it in

Airships were able to carry a small amount of defensive armament. This was most often a number of Maxim machine-guns that could be positioned either within the gondola or on the top platform

During any action, silence and darkness were rigidly maintained throughout the Zeppelin crew

Flight Sub-Lieutenant Reginald Alexander John Warneford VC, RNAS was the first person to successfully bring down an enemy airship on 7 June 1915. He died 10 days later

There were a total of 51 German airship raids over England between 1915 and 1918. During those raids more than 5,000 bombs were dropped killing 557 civilians and injuring 1,358

The largest German airship raid on England took place on the night of 2 September and involved 14 airships. Between them they dropped 261 high explosive and 202 incendiary bombs of the east of the country, killing 4 civilians and causing dozens of injuries

The first airship raid on London took place on 31 May 1915. LZ38 dropped a ton of bombs over the city, killing 7 with another 35 more injured

Zeppelin L32 was classified as a 'Super Zeppelin'. It was 198 metres long, boasted 6 Mayback engines and was capable of 60mph. It was commissioned in August 1916 but made only 11 flights

The first raid using a 'Super Zeppelin' took place over London on the night of 2/3 September 1916 when 16 airships flew towards London. One of the airships, SL11, was intercepted and shot down over Tottenham by Lieutenant William Leefe Robinson of the Royal Flying Corps

Thousands of people witnessed the destruction of SL11; the explosion could be seen 35 miles away. Lt Leefe Robinson was awarded the Victoria Cross for his action

As well as the VC, Lt Leefe Robinson was awarded £4,200 in prize money, an enormous amount of money at that time

Britain had its own airship programme and operated 220 airships at its peak for scouting and reconnaissance

Aces

The term 'Ace' originated in World War I when French newspapers described Adolphe Pègoud as *l'as* (French for ace) after he shot down 5 German aircraft

To become a British 'Ace' a British fighter pilot had to score 5 kills. It was the same for French and American pilots

To qualify as an 'Ace' in the German air force and win the Pour le Mérite medal, a pilot had to score 8 kills

A confirmed 'kill' needed to be independently witnessed to provide proof; however this was often hard to do, especially over enemy lines

Dividing up 'kills' between pilots differed by air force. If more than one member of the US Amy Air Service combined to bring down an enemy machine, they were each awarded the kill. Other forces, including the RFC/RAF divided the kill into fractions, depending on the number of pilots involved

All air forces scored the shooting down of a balloon or an airship as equal to that of shooting down an enemy plane

The most successful fighter of the entire war was Rittmeister Manfred von Richthofen (1892-1918). He shot down 80 planes, more than any other WWI pilot

Richthofen earned the nickname the 'Red Baron' due to his bright red fighter planes that he flew in

In January 1917, after his 16th confirmed 'kill', Richthofen received the Pour le Mérite

'Kills' were often claimed by multiple pilots and even ground crews, especially as the war progressed and the air became more crowded with planes from all sides

The most successful Allied pilot was France's René Fonck (1894-1953) shooting down 75 enemy planes

Another prominent French 'Ace' was Charles Nungesser who

painted a skull, crossbones and a coffin on his aircraft. He received severe injuries but survived the war with 43 confirmed kills, only to be killed trying to fly the Atlantic in May 1927

The top American 'Ace' was Eddie Rickenbacker with 26 confirmed kills

British pilots who scored 8 kills were entitled to the Distinguished Flying Cross

The Australian Flying Corps produced 43 'Aces' all of whom accumulated 5 or more aerial victories

The highest scoring AFC pilot was Captain Arthur 'Harry' Cobby who earned 29 confirmed victories

Cobby was awarded the Distinguished Flying Cross in May 1918 and two further awards of the DFC in September that year. The Distinguished Service Order followed in November 1918

Captain Cobby was the only Australian credited with downing 5 enemy balloons

Australia's leading 'Ace' was Robert Little who registered 47 victories whilst flying with the Royal Naval Air Service

Across all air forces, only 12 'Aces' could boast more than 50 kills during the war

Belgian air crews produced 3 'Aces' during the war

72 American pilots became 'Aces'

The Royal Flying Corps/ Royal Air Force/Royal Naval Air Service

In 1914 the Royal Flying Corps numbered 1,844 men. By November 1918 it had been renamed to the Royal Air Force and had grown to over 300,000

During the Battle of the Somme, the Royal Flying Corps lost 800 aircraft and 252 aircrew killed

The RFC claimed some 7,054 German aircraft and balloons either destroyed, sent 'down out of control' or 'driven down'

The Royal Air Force was formed on 1 April 1918, unifying the Military and Naval roles of the Royal Flying Corps and Royal Navy Air Service into a solitary independent service

In August 1914 the Royal Flying Corps had 50 frontline planes; by June 1918 the RAF had 2,630 operational machines

During 'Bloody April' the average life expectancy of British pilots was 23 days

More British pilots died in flying accidents than in combat during the war

Over 20,000 Canadians served with the RFC & RAF during the war

The Royal Naval Air Service (RNAS) had 93 aircraft, 6 airships and 720 staff at the outbreak of war. By the time it had been amalgamated into the Royal Air Force in 1918 it had 55,000 personnel, 3,000 planes and 103 airships

The most famous RNAS unit was B Flight, Naval 10 Squadron, otherwise known as the Black Flight. Made up of 5 Sopwith Triplanes painted black, each plane was given a name: Black Prince, Black Maria, Black Death, Black Roger and Black Sheep

The pilots of the Black Flight were all Canadian and led by Flight Commander Raymond Collishaw

The Black Flight was credited with 87 'kills' during the summer of 1917 and although they didn't enjoy a great deal of publicity, the Black Flight earned a great reputation with their German counterparts

The Royal Flying Corps decided not to issue their pilots with parachutes because they thought that this would encourage them to bail out of their distressed plane rather than try to bring it home safely

The only British airmen to be issued with parachutes as a piece of standard equipment were the crews of observation balloons as they were so vulnerable to attacks from the ground and from planes

Observation balloons were used to watch enemy activity behind the front lines or to help co-ordinate artillery fire

Observation balloons were tethered to the ground by wires attached to a winch and positioned behind the front lines. There was a wicker basket that was slung beneath the balloon where the crew would view enemy lines or check the accuracy of artillery fire

Communication from observation balloons to the ground was initially via semaphore flags or by weighted messages dropped to the ground before portable radio kits were available

Some balloons were linked together with chains from which wires dangled to trap and damage attacking aircraft – often these groups were positioned over cities or manufacturing plants

Observation balloons were also used to spot enemy submarines and operated in large numbers across the English Channel and the Irish Sea

During the war, Britain produced approximately 5,400 Sopwith Camel fighter planes

Australian Flying Corps

Australia was the only country of the British Empire that formed its own flying corps in World War 1

The Australian Flying Corps (AFC) was officially founded in 1914 and augmented the RFC/RAF contribution in a number of theatres of war

Due to severe shortages of aircraft and instructors the Australian Flying Corps could only accept 2,700 men

Another 200 Australians served directly in the British Royal Flying Corps and the Royal Naval Air Service

The Australian Flying Corps consisted of four squadrons that mostly flew under RFC control until 1918 when it reverted back to its own units

In total, the AFC achieved a total of over 400 confirmed aerial victories

The AFC suffered 175 dead, 111 wounded, 6 gassed and 40 men taken prisoner

German Luftstreikrafte

The German Luftstreikrafte had 250 operational planes at the beginning of the war. By June 1918 they had approximately 2,500

Jasta (squadron) 11 was the highest scoring jasta of the war, with 350 accredited victories

Jasta 11 scored 89 victories during April 1917, one third of the total British losses during that month

Jasta 11's first victory was scored by Manfred von Richthofen on 23 January 1917

In January 1917 the fighter 'Ace' Manfred von Richthofen took control of the fighter squadron Jasta 11 which included some of the elite German pilots

At the same time as Richthofen took control of Jasta 11 he painted his Albatross D.III bright red – earning him the nickname the 'Red Baron'

Richthofen flew a number of planes during the war. The most famous plane being the Fokker Dr.1 triplane, however only 19 of his 80 kills were made in this plane

After his first confirmed victory, Richthofen ordered a silver cup engraved with the date and the type of enemy machine from a jeweller in Berlin. He continued this until he had 60 cups, by which time the dwindling supply of silver in blockaded Germany meant that silver cups like this could no longer be supplied

Altogether, 26 'Aces' flew in Jasta 11 including Hermann Goering

In late June 1917 Manfred von Richthofen took command of the first ever German Jagdgeschwader (fighter group). It was nicknamed the Flying Circus due to the garish colours each plane was painted plus the fact that much of their supplies and equipment remained packed ready for quick transportation via rail to areas of the front where they were needed

Jadgdeschwader 1 was made up of Jastas 4, 6, 10 and 11

On 6 July 1917, Richthofen sustained a serious head-wound during a dog fight, knocking him out and causing partial sight loss. He regained consciousness in time to ease the aircraft out of a free-falling spin and executed a rough landing in a field

By 1918 the Red Baron had become a national hero in Germany and he was used by the German propaganda machine to motivate other troops and the civilian population

German propaganda even issued false rumours and news about Richthofen, for example that the British had formed special hunting squadrons specifically to shoot down Richthofen and had offered a large reward and an instant Victoria Cross to the man who successfully brought him down

Richthofen was fatally wounded by ground fire just after 11:00am on 21 April 1918, while flying over Morlancourt Ridge, near the Somme River

Richthofen was buried with full military honours in the cemetery at the village of Bertangles, near Amiens, on 22 April 1918 by the personnel of No. 3 Squadron Australian Flying Corps

French Aèronautique Militaire

In August 1914 the French Aèronautique Militaire had 132 front line planes

By the end of the war, the French could call upon 3,222 front line machine plus thousands more in reserve and training roles

French personnel also increased greatly during the war; from about 8,000 in May 1915 to 52,000 towards the end of 1918

The French Aèronautique Militaire was split into three groups: general reconnaissance and artillery spotting duties were assigned to corps squadrons (*escadrilles de corps*); there were fighter squadrons (*escadrilles de chasse*) and bombing squadrons (*escadrilles de bombardment*)

The French Aèronautique Militaire lost some 3,700 aircraft during the war, 2,000 of which were lost in 1918

Increased manufacturing output of French machines resulted in 400-500 new machines being delivered every month to the front line by the end of 1916

This improved output meant that by the time of the Battle of Verdun the French Aèronautique Militaire had 1,149 machines ready for action at the front line

Although this was an impressive number, only 135 of those planes were fighters with another 188 bombers

By the time of the Armistice the French Aèronautique Militaire was able to boast a total of 3,222 front line aircraft along with thousands of reserve and training machines along with 127,630 officers and men including more than 12,000 pilots

One elite French fighter group was nicknamed *Les Cigognes* (the storks). Each escadrille painted a different version of the stork symbol on their planes

The French naval air service in 1914 could muster just 8 machines and 200 men. By the end of the war it had more than 1,250 aircraft, over 250 balloons and 11,000 personnel

Anti-Aircraft Weapons

The first purpose designed anti-aircraft weapons were converted German field guns and were operational in 1909

Anti-aircraft artillery guns were known as 'Archie' to the British soldiers

All anti-aircraft guns were either controlled by navies or by army artillery, except for Germany where the German Army Air Service was in control off A-A fire

By 1914, the French army had 2 operational purpose built anti-aircraft armoured cars carrying their famous 'Soixante Quinze' field gun

Both sides fired artillery rounds into the air that released smoke clouds and shrapnel into the air on explosion. The British forces nicknamed these guns 'Archie'

Aircraft Balloons were particularly vulnerable as hydrogen (which was used to inflate them) is extremely flammable. Both sides used special incendiary bullets to exploit this

6. THE WAR AT SEA

General

The Battle of Jutland took place at the end of May 1916 and was the largest naval battle of the war

During the Battle of Jutland the Royal Navy lost 3 battle cruisers, 3 cruisers, and 8 destroyers, with the loss of 6,097 killed.

The German High Seas Fleet lost 1 pre-Dreadnought, 1 battle cruiser, 4 light cruisers and 5 destroyers, with 2,551 casualties killed

RMS *Lusitania*, a British cruise liner was torpedoed and sunk 11 miles off the southern coast of Ireland by U-20 killing 1,198 people including 128 Americans. This sinking caused huge anti-German feelings in America

The oil tanker *Gulflight* was the first US ship to be attacked by German U-boats when it was torpedoed by U-30 on 1 May 1915

There were no modern day aircraft carriers in service during the war. Instead a number of fast passenger liners were converted as seaplane tenders. These were capable of transporting and launching planes, but not for landing

Italy's first naval loss of the war was *Amalfi* a large armoured cruiser which was torpedoed by U-14 on 7 July 1915 in the northern Adriatic

The French navy lost 166 vessels during the war, including four battleships (*Bouvet, Danton, Gaulois* and *Suffren*)

By the end of the war the French navy had almost 1,300 vessels in service. Mostly small craft that were used for minesweeping and anti-submarine duties

The Italian navy was the acknowledged world leader in operating successful coastal torpedo boats at the beginning of the war

One of the most spectacular Italian torpedo boat successes of the war came on 10 June 1918 where a pair of their torpedo boats attacked and sank the Austrian dreadnought *Szent István* in the northern Adriatic. The dreadnought sank within 3 hours

The psychological damage to the Austro-Hungarian navy following the sinking of the *Szent István* was so great that their fleet never put to sea again during the war

The opening shots of the Battle of Jutland commenced at a distance of 16,500 yards

In 1914 the Russian fleet consisted of 30 ships with a displacement of over 6,000 tons including 11 battleships, and 6 dreadnought battle cruisers

As well as these big ships, in 1914 the Russian navy boasted 25 submarines, 81 torpedo boat destroyers and 18 torpedo boats

The Russian naval fleet suffered a number of mutinies in 1915

In 1917 the Russian Baltic fleet helped ensure the success of the Bolshevik revolution. The cruiser *Aurora* fired a blank shell on the Winter Palace and raised the red flag on 7 November

The Russian navy were mainly occupied in the Baltic Sea, trying to deny German access to Petrograd

By the end of 1915 Russian minelayers had laid more than 3,000 mines in the Baltic in an effort to block German efforts to interfere with Russian trade routes to Scandinavia

After the Russian Revolution and the general collapse of the Russian armed forces, the Russian Baltic fleet escaped to the Gulf of Finland where it remained until the war in the Baltic was finished

Brazil cut all diplomatic relations with Germany on 11 April 1917 after a Brazilian steamer was sunk off of Cherbourg

Another Brazilian ship, *Tijuca*, was torpedoed on 20 May by a German U-boat led to the seizure of all 42 German merchant ships that were in Brazilian ports

The French navy completed just 3 dreadnought class battleships during the war. The *Bretagne*, *Provence* and *Lorraine* were ordered in 1912, almost completed by August 1914 but construction was paused. *Provence* was eventually completed in mid-1915 and all three were in service by autumn 1916

The Canadian navy was founded in 1910 but was denied any investment pre-war and as such was a tiny force with just 2 obsolete cruisers and 2 submarines in 1914

Canada did add vessels to their navy during the war and by the Armistice there were over 5,000 men in naval service

Another 3,000 Canadians enlisted with the Royal Navy

A depth charge was a waterproof bomb based on delayed action shells. They were used by Allied navies from 1915

Very few were carried at first and by the end of 1917 only 9 U-boats had been destroyed by depth charge

In 1918 they were manufactured in greater numbers. This, along with a new firing mechanism that ensured they were pushed far away from the ship that was firing them, meant that they accounted for 22 U-boat losses in the final year of war

U-boats and Submarines

The largest pre-war submarine fleet belonged to France. They were able to boast 120 vessels, however many of them were not fit for active war service

At the outbreak of war the German Navy possessed the most advanced submarine service in the war, but even they only had ten working boats capable of taking on a warship, with another 18 older boats being used for training and coastal defence

Early U-boats were slow, had no surface guns and were slow to dive, making them vulnerable to enemy attack. As a consequence many traditional Germany officers were sceptical of their value

The term U-boat is derived from the German *unterseeboot*, (literally under sea boat) and was used by all Allied countries to describe all German submarines although the U prefix was only officially used for the larger, long range craft as opposed to the smaller UB and UC classes

Germany's war time U-boats can be organised into 7 distinct types: boats for export, gasoline boats, ocean going diesel powered attack boats, merchant boats, coastal torpedo attack boats, UC ocean minelayers and UE coastal minelayers

The largest ship sunk by U-boats was HMRS *Britannic*. It was sunk on 21 November 1916 in the Aegean Sea after hitting a mine laid by U-73. The 48,158 tonne ship sunk in 55 minutes

By the end of the war a total of 375 German U-boats had been commissioned

7,646 Allied ships were hit (sunk/damaged/captured) by U-boats between 1914 and 1918

The notion of the 'Ace' was also used with regards to German U-boat commanders although the system was less developed than that used for pilots. Those commanders who sunk large amounts of Allied merchant shipping or enemy warships were included

The British answer to the U-boat was the 'E' boats. These were well armed with 5 torpedo tubes and a decent deck gun. They also had good surface speed, but mechanically they were less reliable than their German counterparts

One 'E' boat, E-11, commanded by Lt-Commander Martin Nasmith was very successful in sinking 27 steamers and 58 other vessels over 3 patrols in the Dardenelles in 1915

On long journeys many submarine commanders had to rely on carrier pigeon for communications

The Royal Navy had the largest Allied fleet of submarines at the end of the war with 137 serving boats, with another 78 under construction

One of the reasons why Allied submarines were not as successful as German U-boats was that the blockaded Central Powers simply didn't have enough merchant ships to be hunted.

The Royal Navy suffered 54 lost submarines during the war

The first British warship sunk by a U-Boat was HMS *Pathfinder*, who was sunk by a torpedo fired by U-1 near St Abbs Head. She sunk in 4 minutes

The UC mine laying boats were designed specifically for laying small minefields that were very difficult to see. Introduced in the summer of 1915, they were a very effective naval weapon, sinking more than a million tonnes of Allied shipping during the war

A second version of the UC mine laying boats was introduced in 1916. They could carry 18 mines over 11,000km and had an 88mm gun for surface attacks

In 1917 U-boats accounted for the sinking of 2,439 Allied merchant ships

German wartime U-boat losses were significant – 192 boats were lost along with over 5,400 crew members

On 5 June 1916 the British Armoured Cruiser, HMS *Hampshire*, struck a mine laid by U-boats off of the Orkneys. She sank in a matter of minutes with the loss of 643 lives, including Lord Kitchener, the British Minister of War

Germany had 10 shipyards in operation dedicated to building U-boats

The most successful U-boat of the war (based on tonnage sunk) was U35 which accounted for 226 ships with a grand total of 538,498 tonnes

During the war the Royal Navy lost 2 dreadnoughts, 3 battle cruisers, 11 battleships, 25 cruisers, 54 submarines, 64 destroyers and 10 torpedo boats

A submerged British submarine sunk U-40 off the coast of Aberdeen in June 1915

The Royal Navy

At the outbreak of war, Britain and France entered an agreement that the Royal Navy would operate in the North Sea and Atlantic and the French navy would operate in the Mediterranean

The entire Dardenelles submarine campaign was perhaps the only successful part of the whole Dardenelles campaign and resulted for 2 battleships, 1 destroyer, 5 gunboats, 7 supply ships, 9 troop carriers, 35 steamers and 188 various other ships

Room 40 was the name given to the secret Royal Navy intelligence department that, from December 1914, worked to decipher German radio messages

A total of 16,500 depth charges were used by the Royal Navy during the war

HMS *Dreadnought* was launched in December 1906 and with her bigger, longer range guns and bigger better engines rendered every other current battleship sailing the seas obsolete

HMS *Dreadnought* carried twenty-two 12 pounder guns; each could achieve a rate of fire of 15 rounds per minute. She could also reach a top speed of 22 knots, faster than any of her rivals at that time

The appearance of HMS *Dreadnought* sent the world's navies into mild panic and sparked off a naval arms race, especially with Germany

The Royal Navy launched 23 more Dreadnought class battleships up until 1914 and launched another 11 during the war itself

Germany built and launched 17 before the war and managed another 2 during hostilities

HMS *Dreadnought* did not take part in the Battle of Jutland as she was being refitted at the time

Throughout the war, HMS *Dreadnought* sank 1 enemy U-boat – U-29 in 1915

Germany ended the war with its entire fleet of Dreadnoughts in-tact, the Royal Navy lost only two (HMS *Audacious* and HMS *Vanguard*)

Britain developed and produced a number of coastal torpedo boats, mostly designed by the Thornycroft engineering company

At the beginning of the war Britain could boast over 300 destroyers. Germany had 144

During the war Germany produced 107 more destroyers, but Britain managed to construct another 329

The main role of the destroyer was to protect larger warships such as the dreadnoughts from torpedo boats and submarines/U-boats

At the Battle of Jutland, Britain committed 73 destroyers to the fight, whereas Germany threw 61 of her destroyer contingent into the fighting

The Allies lost 112 destroyers during the war, with over 50% of losses suffered by the Royal Navy

The Central Powers lost 62 destroyers – 53 of which were German

The British Royal Naval Air Service were early pioneers in attempts to use large ships as floating air-fields. The first seaplane tender was a converted cruiser; HMS *Hermes*

HMS *Hermes* was sunk by torpedo in October 1914

The first aircraft carrier was HMS *Ark Royal*, an ex-collier that had been converted to carry planes and entered service in December 1914

The Royal Navy also converted a number of passenger ferries to carry planes. The ferries relative high cruising speed was important in allowing them to keep up with other warships in the fleet

These early converted ships could launch planes into the air, but didn't have sufficient 'runway' to accept incoming planes. These had to be winched out of the sea

The first ever sea-based air raid was launched against Zeppelin hangars near Cuxhaven on 25 December 1914

HMS *Furious* was a former light battle cruiser but was converted to carry planes in late 1917. She was able to carry 3 short 184 Seaplanes and 5 Sopwith Pup fighters

Despite having a second flight deck installed landing on HMS *Furious* was virtually impossible due to turbulence from its central superstructure and funnels

HMS *Furious* took part in the Tondern Raid of 18 July 1918 which was a British attack against a Zeppelin base on the Dutch-German border. It was the first time aircraft were launched from an aircraft carrier. Out of the 5 planes that took part in the raid, 3 were forced to ditch in the sea rather than land on the carrier, 2 made it to neutral Denmark and one plane was lost

HMS *Argus* was the first flat deck carrier which from which planes could take off and land. She was a converted passenger liner and entered service in October 1918

The first purpose built aircraft carrier was HMS *Hermes*, but she did not see any war action

In 1914 the only effective means of attacking submarines and U-boats were mines laid at various depths along known routes

Such underwater mines accounted for at least 75 boats. British mines accounted for 48 confirmed sinkings

Q-Ships were decoy vessels deployed by Allied navies as anti-submarine weapons. They sailed disguised as unarmed merchant ships but actually hosted up to 4 deck guns

The first British Q-Ships entered service in November 1914; eventually the Royal Navy had over 350 Q-Ships in service

61 British Q-Ships were lost during the war

British Q-Ships accounted for 11 U-Boats

As well as in the Royal Navy, Q-Ships were employed in the French, Russian and Italian navies

The German navy had their own version of Q-Ships. Auxiliary

Commerce Raiders were German warships disguised as unarmed merchant vessels. They flew neutral flags and targeted Allied surface shipping

Most Auxiliary Commerce Raiders were minelayers converted to look like merchant vessels. It is estimated that a dozen or so ships were operated

The Royal Navy used trawlers to tow submerged submarines that were ready to surface and attack any enemy vessel that got too close

The German Navy

The German cruiser *Emden* sunk 23 Allied vessels during the war

The German Navy scuttled 51 warships at Scapa Flow on 21 June 1919

The German battleship *Baden* was the last battleship built in Germany during the war. It was completed in October 1916; she served as the flagship of the German High Seas fleet from 1917 until the Armistice

As it became clear that after Jutland there would be no more big naval battles, two Baden class battleships, the *Sachsen* and *Württenberg* were abandoned whilst still undergoing construction in 1917

By early 1916 German naval losses in the Baltic region were three times that of Russian naval losses

7. BATTLES

1914

Following the battle of Mons and the retreat to Le Cateau *The Times* newspaper printed its 'Amiens Dispatch' on 30 August 1914. It was somewhat despondent in its tone and dulled significantly the jubilant mood back home in Britain

The total British casualties amounted to just over 1,600 of all ranks, killed, wounded and missing, during the Battle of Mons

Practically half of these were from just 2 battalions (400 of the 4th Middlesex and 300 of the 2nd Royal Irish)

German losses during Battle of Mons are believed to have been in excess of 5,000

During the Brusilov offensive 581 Austro-Hungarian artillery guns were captured

When the Russian army captured the fortress town of Przemysl on 22 March 1915 approximately 120,000 Austro-Hungarians surrendered and 700 heavy guns were captured

When the Germans captured the fortress of Novogeorgievsk the Russians lost 1,600 guns

During the Battle of Mons in 1914, the small but highly trained BEF fended off a much larger German force with fire from their Short Magazine Lee Enfield (SMLE) rifles. The fire was so intense the Germans were convinced they were facing machine-guns

The Battle of Tannenberg (23-30 August 1914) didn't actually take place in Tannenberg, but 20 miles to the west, in a town called Allenstein. It was decided by the German High Command after the event to call it such in an effort to erase the memory of the original battle in 1410 when the Teutonic Knights were beaten by the Poles and Lithuanians

In the 7 days of the 1914 Battle of Tannenberg the German Army took 95,000 Russian prisoners, practically destroying the Russian 2nd Army

After the battle, General Samsonov, commander of the Russian Second Army, committed suicide

The German army expended more ammunition during the three day Battle of the Marne in 1914 than the Prussian army had used throughout the entire Franco-Prussian War of 1870-71

In an attempt to keep the Germans out of Flanders during the First Battle of Ypres, sluice gates were opened that caused the North Sea to flood the flat plains of Flanders

Kaiser Wilhelm was so confident of victory at Ypres he travelled to the town anticipating to lead his troops through the town on a victory march

On 11 November 1914 the elite Prussian Guard threw themselves at Ypres in a last ditch attempt to win the town. The situation was so bad that cooks, orderlies and other support staff picked up rifles to defend the lines

Britain suffered around 54,000 casualties during the First Battle of Ypres

The First Battle of Ypres between 14 October and 22 November 1914 practically destroyed the BEF as a legitimate fighting force

French and Belgian casualties were approximately 59,000. Germany suffered in excess of 100,000 casualties

173 German heavy guns opened fire on to the forts of Antwerp on 28 September 1914. The town of Antwerp surrendered on 9 October 1914

Antwerp was under constant German occupation from 9 October 1914 until late in 1918

The first action on the Mesopotamian Front was the battle of Basra which began on 5 November 1914 and involved 5,000 troops from the Indian Army

Anglo-Indian troops finally occupied Basra on 23 November 1914

1915

During the battle of Loos on 25 September 1915 troops from the 47th (London) Division created an army of wooden soldiers which they moved about within a gas and smoke barrage. Across No Man's Land the German defenders were not sure if they were being attacked and wasted significant manpower and resources firing on these dummies. Called a 'Chinese attack' the diversion was successful and over time was widely adopted

The Battle of Loos was the first time the British army had used gas in war and was also the first time Lord Kitchener's New Armies would see action on the Western Front

During the landings on the Gallipoli peninsular, 17,000 ANZAC troops were dropped off at the wrong beach. Instead of landing at Gaba Tepe they ended up a mile north at the much smaller cape surrounded by sheer cliffs called Ari Burnu

Between 10 and 20 December 1915 105,000 men and 300 guns were successfully evacuated from Anzac Cove and Sulva Bay. Another 35,000 men were evacuated from Helles in late December and early January 1917

In the final stage of the evacuation of the Gallipoli peninsula 3,689 horses and mules were safely extracted from the war zone

The first large scale gas attack, launched on 22 April 1915 by Germany, signalled the beginning of the Second Battle of Ypres

During the Second Battle of Ypres Britain lost 59,275 casualties (killed, missing or wounded) – 6,341 of those were Canadians

French and Belgian casualties during the Second Battle of Ypres totalled approximately 11,500

German casualties during the Second Battle of Ypres was 34,933

During the battle of Loos in 1915 one German machine gun was reported to have fired 12,000 bullets

When ordered to take part in the first attack in the Battle of Loos in September 1915, units of the 47th (London) Division left a portion of the officers, NCOs and men behind. The idea was that they would form a cadre on which the unit could be rebuilt if it suffered very heavy losses. This gradually became a standard practice for all Divisions on the Western Front

The codename for the Austro-Hungarian attack on Russia which began on 27 August 1915 was the 'Black-Yellow' offensive

The 'Black-Yellow' offensive started positively but was abandoned within a month. The Austro-Hungarian army had suffered 300,000 casualties in that time

1916

The Battle of the Somme was originally meant to be a French led offensive with the British in support. It was also initially planned for August 1916

When the Germany army attacked Verdun in February 1916 it was clear that France would not be able to lead any major offensive, indeed a British attack was needed fast to take the pressure of the French and divert German resources away from Verdun

In the preliminary artillery bombardment for the Battle of the Somme, British artillery fired 1.73 million shells on to the German lines

Many of the shells that were fired in the preliminary bombardment were duds and failed to explode, those that did explode tended to be shrapnel shells and not high explosive (HE) shells and as a consequence had little effect on barbed wire defences, dugouts and enemy strong points

Britain lost 57,470 casualties (killed and wounded) on the first day of the Battle of the Somme (1 July 1916)

The average British infantryman carried 30kg of equipment as he went over the top during the first phase of the Battle of the Somme

In the advance on the Somme, the British infantry was ordered to advance towards the enemy trenches at 3.2kph – walking pace

The oldest soldier to die during the first day of the Battle of the Somme was Lt Henry Webber 7th South Lancashire aged 68, he joined to serve with his 3 sons who all survived

During the battle of Flers-Courcelette on 15 September 1916 the tank made its operational debut. Although they scared many of the German soldiers in the front line a mixture of poor tactics and unreliability meant that overall they failed to make a great impact

During the Battle of the Somme, 51 Victoria Crosses were awarded – 17 of them were awarded posthumously

The battle of Verdun caused almost 1 million casualties, making it one of the most deadly battles in history

During the battle of Verdun it is estimated that over 32 million artillery shells were fired

Approximately half of all casualties of Verdun were killed

During the fighting in the Somme region of France between July and November 1916, the French and British armies suffered around 615,000 casualties

During the Brusilov offensive the Russian advance took 417,000 Austro-Hungarian prisoners

In addition 581 Austro-Hungarian guns were captured by Brusilov's offensive

During the preliminary bombardment before the Australians attacked towards the villages of Fleurbaix and Fromelles the maps the officers were using were out of date. The German lines were actually 200m further away than they thought. As a consequence the 200,000 shells that were fired in that bombardment fell harmlessly into No Man's Land

With defences and positions intact the Germans were able to cause massive casualties to the advancing troops. The Australians lost 5,533 men in just 1 day. The Australian War Memorial describes the battle of Fromelles as 'the worst 24 hours in Australia's entire history'

1917

The preliminary bombardment for the Second Battle of the Aisne opened up on 2 April. A month later over 5,000 French guns had fired 11 million shells

On the first day of the Second Battle of the Aisne (16 April 1917) the French Fifth and Sixth Armies attacked along an 80km front against heavily fortified German defences

The French armies suffered approximately 40,000 casualties and lost around 150 tanks

The French attacks during the Second Battle of the Aisne continued until 9 May and employed 1.2million men and 7,000 guns

The Second Battle of Aisne cost the French Army around 187,000 casualties and it cost General Nivelle his job. The Third Battle of Ypres, launched on 31 July 1917 is better known as the Battle of Passchendaele

The preliminary bombardment for the Battle of Passchendaele lasted 10 days and included more than 3,000 guns of various calibre, firing some 4.25 million shells

Canadian forces finally took the village of Passchendaele on 6 November 1917

The Battle of Passchendaele cost the Allies about 310,000 casualties

In the 10 day preliminary bombardment of the Third Battle of Ypres, the Allies fired 4,250,000 artillery shells

During 100 days of fighting the Third Battle of Ypres, the Allies managed to advance a little over 5 miles

The average daily British advance during the Third Battle of Ypres between 31 July and 7 December 1917 was 68 yards

The Allies used over 3,000 artillery guns of various shapes and sizes during the Third Battle of Ypres

The Battle of Cambrai started on 20 November 1917. After the disaster of Passchendaele, Field Marshall Haig was desperate to finish the year on a positive note

The Battle of Cambrai was the first battle in history where tanks were used in large numbers to spearhead an offensive

324 British tanks were used in the initial assault

On the first day of battle, the much vaunted Hindenburg Line had been broken, but 179 tanks had been lost

Of the 179 tank losses on the first day of battle, 65 were destroyed by the enemy, 43 were ditched and 71 suffered mechanical failure

The success of the first day resulted in the ringing of church bells across Britain

As the battle began the British smashed the German defensive positions with 1,003 artillery guns

Despite initial successes, within 1 week the Germans had recaptured most of the early lost ground

Anglo-Indian troops captured Baghdad, the southern capital of the then Ottoman Empire in March 1917. British troops occupied the city on 11 March 1917 and were noisily welcomed by the Baghdad population

Turkish losses whilst trying to defend Baghdad is estimated to be between 25,000 and 30,000 men

The loss of Baghdad practically ended the Turkish activity in Persia

The disaster for Italy at Caporetto in October 1917 and the following withdrawal of to the Piave River cost the Italian army around 300,000 men killed, missing and wounded. In addition they lost 3,150 artillery pieces, 3,000 machine guns and 300,000 rifles

1918

Kaiserschlacht was the German name given to the large spring offensives launched on the Western Front during the spring of 1918

The first phase of the Kaiserschlacht was Operation Michael. It was to be the main attack, led by elite storm troopers and was meant to push the British back over the old Somme battlefields, back towards the coast

Operation Michael was launched on 21 March 1918

In the preliminary bombardment 6,600 artillery guns fired over 1 million shells in just over 5 hours over a 90km front from Arras to La Fére

The British suffered 7,500 casualties in this bombardment. The front and support lines were thrown into complete chaos

By the end of the first day both German and British casualties were in the region of 40,000 each, with the British Army in full retreat

By 25 March the British Fifth Army, located in the south of the front line, had been forced to retreat almost 40 miles west

The German advance during the early stages of Operation Michael was so spectacular and so ominous that the Kaiser decorated Hindenburg with the Iron Cross with Golden Rays, last awarded to Prince Blücher after the Battle of Waterloo

Despite the massive advances, the German losses were huge at almost 250,000 casualties. The remaining troops quickly became exhausted and outstripped supply lines – the advance soon petered out

The second phase of Kaiserschlacht was known as Operation Georgette or the Battle of Lys and had the objective of capturing the high ground of Mont Kemmel and drive the British Army out of the Ypres Salient towards the coast

Operation Georgette commenced on the 9 April, the Germans advanced 3 miles on the first day

The third phase of the Kaiserschlacht offensive was called Operation Blücher-Yorck otherwise known as the Third Battle of the Aisne. It was a direct attack on Paris in an effort to draw British troops out of Ypres

4,000 guns were involved in the preliminary bombardment which commenced on 27 May 1918

By the end of the first day the Germans had advanced up to 10 miles in many places. By 3 June they were only 55 miles from Paris

Casualties for Operation Blücher-Yorck were heavy for all sides. France suffered 98,000 casualties, Britain lost 29,000 and although German losses are not known it is thought they were around 130,000 – men killed, missing or wounded

The fourth and final phase of the Kaiserschlacht offensive was called Operation Gneisenau and was engineered to flatten out the salient created by Blücher-Yorck

Confessions from prisoners and diligent work by French code breakers meant that the Allies knew about the advance in good time to prepare sufficiently

The infantry advance of Operation Gneisenau took place on 8 June 1918. This was preceded by a massive bombardment including 750,000 gas shells

On the first day of the attack the Germans advanced more than 5 miles and took 8,000 prisoners

By 10 June the Germans were just 45 miles from Paris

Operation Gneisenau was halted by a joint Franco/American counter attack which included 150 tanks

During the battle of Bellau Wood the Americans were drafted in to help out the beleaguered French. Soon after they arrived, the American troops were strongly urged to fall back in line with the French, to which, Captain Lloyd W. Williams of the 2nd Battalion, 5th Marines uttered the now famous riposte, "Retreat? Hell, we just got here."

Allied casualties (killed, missing, wounded) for the Battle of Amiens was approximately 22,000

Germany lost 30,000 casualties (killed, missing, wounded) plus another 20,000 men taken prisoner on 8 August 1918, the first day of the Battle of Amiens

Such huge losses led Ludendorff to remark that this day was 'the black day of the German Army'

The Battle of Amiens heralded the start of the Allied 'Hundred Days Offensive' which resulted in the final defeat of Germany and the end of the war

Over 1,900 Allied planes were used during the Battle of Amiens

The Battle of Amiens began on 8 August 1918 in an effort to flatten out a large salient (bulge in the line) in that area

The main front of attack stretched out across 22km

The German defenders standing in the way of the Allied advance during the Battle of Amiens numbered less than 20,000. They were outnumbered 6:1

British infantry in the attack were supported by 2,070 artillery pieces smashing the German front and reserve lines

Canadian and Australian troops advanced 12km by the afternoon

To help them the depleted German forces could only count on 365 operational airplanes to help them

At the end of the Battle of Amiens the British had only 6 operational tanks left out of a starting force of 500

8. COMBATANTS: BRITAIN & THE COMMONWEALTH

The size of the British Expeditionary Force (BEF) was about 120,000 in 1914

'Tommy Atkins' is the shorthand name for the average British soldier in uniform

The original BEF was equipped and trained for a mobile war, they didn't have great quantities of artillery, mortars or machine-guns

In his 'Order of the Day' on 19 August 1914, Kaiser Wilhelm II urged his troops to 'walk over General French's contemptible little army.' From that day on, the British Expeditionary Force from 1914 would be forever known as 'The Old Contemptibles'

On 22 August 1914, Corporal E. Thomas of the 4th Troop, 4th Royal Irish Dragoon Guards fired the first British shot of the war whilst on a forward patrol near Maisières

In 1925 Captain John Patrick Danny of the Royal Field Artillery founded The Old Contemptible Association for veterans of the BEF

The average age of the original BEF was 30

Many recruits were under-nourished and with the regular meals and exercise that came with army life many put on over a stone in weight

Throughout the war Britain and the Commonwealth mobilised around 8,700,000 men

Around 4 million men were recruited during the war years from England, 557,000 from Scotland, 273,000 from Wales and almost 135,000 from Ireland

Almost 5.4 million men from the British and Commonwealth armies served on the Western Front at some point

The second most populated theatre when it came to British troops was Egypt and Palestine with almost 1.2 million men

The peak strength of British and Commonwealth troops on the Western Front was 2,046,901

Compare this with the theatre boasting the second highest concentration of troops – Mesopotamia with 447, 531

The minimum age to volunteer for the British Army was 18

The youngest authenticated soldier of the war was Private Sidney Lewis who joined the East Surrey Regiment in August 1915 aged 12. He went on to serve during the Battle of the Somme aged 13

It is thought that 15% of wartime volunteers were underage

In 1916 the average 'Tommy' carried between 70-90lb of kit

A Tommies' fighting kit weighed about 50-55lb

The daily wage in 1914 for a 'Private' was 1s 0d

The British army employed 300,000 field workers to cook and supply food to the troops

At the beginning of the war British soldiers were 'officially' given 10oz of meat and 8oz of vegetables a day

For minor offenses such as not saluting a senior officer, being unshaven or untidy or being late on parade, the typical punishment was to lose a day's pay or suffer extra fatigue work

For moderate offences such as drunkenness, negligently discharging firearms or disobeying orders the punishment could be up to 28 days in prison or significant fines

For serious offenses such as cowardice, striking an officer, desertion or falling asleep whilst on sentry duty the offender would be tried by court martial, the punishment could be death by firing squad

During the war 5,952 officers were court marshalled, along with 298,310 other ranks. Roughly 3% of the army

Of those tried 89% were found guilty and convicted

3,080 men were sentenced to death (1.1% of those convicted). Of these, 89% were reprieved and the sentence converted to a lesser one

306 men were executed

The first British soldier to be executed was 19-year-old Private Thomas Highgate who was found hiding in a barn wearing civilian clothes on 5 September 1914. He was promptly tried by court martial and found guilty of desertion. He was executed by firing squad at dawn on 8 September 1914

Field punishment number 1 consisted of the convicted man being put in irons and secured to a fixed object for up to 2 hours in 24. This punishment was often known as a crucifixion

Due to the humiliating nature of field punishment number 1, it was despised by the British Tommy

Field punishment number 2 was the same as number 1 but the convicted man was not tied to anything

The British Military Police were responsible for arresting men without passes, or those who robbed and committed other such offensives, as well as collecting stragglers and searching for spies

The British Military Police were given the nickname 'the Redcaps' due to the red cover around their service cap

Edith Cavell (1865-12 October 1915) was a British nurse who saved soldiers from all sides. When she helped 200 Allied soldiers escape from German-occupied Belgium, the Germans arrested her and she was executed by a German firing squad. Her death helped turn global opinion against Germany

306 British and Commonwealth soldiers were executed for crimes such as desertion and cowardice

80,000 British Army soldiers suffered from shell shock over the course of the war

Sir Winston Churchill was sacked from his post as First Lord of the Admiralty on 26 May 1915 after the failure of the Gallipoli campaign

The Flemish town of Ypres, an important communication and transport hub for the British Army and the subject of severe fighting throughout the war, was known as 'Wipers' to the British Tommy

Field Marshall Earl Kitchener of Khartoum became minister of war on 5 August 1915 and immediately put plans together to expand the British Army

Within two weeks of Kitchener's 'Call to Arms', 100,000 men had signed up: Kitchener's first army of volunteers (K1) was born

By the end of September 1914 another 100,000 men had volunteered for service and another army (K2) had been set up

By March 1915, 5 armies were complete and a sixth had been sanctioned by the government

To begin with, the army struggled to kit out these new armies, many men trained in their own clothes or in antiquated uniforms for earlier wars

The Canadian Automobile Machine Gun Brigade No 1, established on 2 September 1914 was the first ever fully mechanised army unit

The first specialist British tunnelling companies were formed as part of the Royal Engineers on 12 February 1915

Civilian men were bombarded with messages urging them to sign up and do their bit for Britain. Postcards, posters, newspapers and even popular songs were written to continue the recruitment drive

The King's Shilling was issued to a recruit when he enlisted into the British Army. It was a symbolic gesture that each new soldier was given his first day's pay – a shilling when he signed up

Each recruit was medically assessed and rated. If you were given the category 'A1' then you were fit for general service; if you were 'B1' you were fit for overseas service and if you were 'C1' then you were deemed fit for home service only

A 'C3' category was given to men who were deemed unfit for service overseas. These men were dubbed 'Category Men'

Groups of females would issue white feathers to men not in uniform. The white feather was a symbol of cowardice

Conscientious Objectors (known as COs or conchies) were men who refused to sign up for military service due to a strong belief that war was wrong

Conscientious Objectors were hounded by the press and given a hard time by the general public

On 2 June 1915 the British government passed the Munitions of War Act which led to the mass employment of women workers. 46,000 women rush to fill gaps in the country's war production industry within one week

Over the course of the war the number of women employed in Britain increased by 2 million

National Registration Act of 1915 required citizens to register their name, address, occupation and date of birth. It immediately identified 3.4 million men who were technically able to join up

By the autumn of 1915 the number of recruits signing on the line was falling through the floor and was no way near the 35,000 a week recommended by Lord Kitchener

The Military Service Act was introduced across Britain on 27 January 1916. With this legislation all voluntary enlistment ceased. All British males between 19 and 41, living in Britain and either unmarried or a widower were now conscripted and deemed to have had joined up on 2 March 1916

Conscripted men did not have a choice as to which service, regiment or unit they joined

With the introduction of the Military Service Act all conscientious objectors were forced to sit before tribunals to argue their case for not going to war

Some men with certain trades or skills were exempt as they were deemed as vital for the war effort. These were called 'starred occupations'

The Military Service Act initially failed to deliver the numbers of men needed. Only 43,000 of the initial draft of men called up actually qualified for service. Another 93,000 failed to turn up to their local recruiting office when asked

748,587 men claimed some form of exemption, filling the tribunal courts

Conscription ceased on 11 November 1918 and all conscripts were discharged, if they had not already been so, on 31 March 1920

In an effort to ensure enough officers a new system of training officers was introduced in February 1916. From then onwards a temporary commission could only be granted if a man had been through an officer cadet unit

Officer training took around 4 and a half months

More than 73,000 men gained infantry commissions after being trained via an officer cadet unit

British field ambulances were mobile medical units and not an actual ambulance in the modern sense

Each British Division had 3 field ambulances as well as a specialist sanitary unit

It was the field ambulances that organised main and advanced dressing stations

These dressing stations were where casualties could receive more treatment and get ready to be sent to a casualty clearing station if needed

Most dressing stations were located in existing buildings, underground dug-outs or bunkers

Dressing stations and field ambulances were run and manned by the Royal Army Medical Corps

The casualty clearing station was a large, static and well equipped medical facility, situated several miles behind the lines with good access to road and rail networks

A typical British casualty clearing station could hold up to 1,000 casualties at any one time

Often made up of tents or huts, these casualty clearing stations were normally grouped together with 3 or 4 stations situated within a couple of miles of each other

In 1916 734,000 wounded men were evacuated from CCSs by train and another 17,000 by canal barge on the Western Front alone

If a case could not be satisfactorily treated in a CSS then they would be transported to a base hospital, either by an ambulance train, motor ambulance or canal barge

There were 2 base hospitals per Division; a typical base hospital could hold 400 casualties each

More than half of those admitted to a base hospital were evacuated to Britain for further treatment or convalescence

Many CSS sites are marked by large military cemeteries today

During the recruitment process, Sportsman's Battalions were allowed to recruit men up to the age of 45 years as it was thought that ex-professional sportsmen were generally more fitter than the average civilian

In October 1918 the 'Feed the Guns' show installed a First World War mock trench in the square, complete with dug-outs, a wooden tank and a bombed out farmhouse, in an effort to raise money for war bonds

During the war, Britain ran out of traditional sheep wool needed for clothing. Dog hair was used instead

The number of men serving in the British Artillery as a percentage of the whole of the British Army rose from 4% in 1914 to 14% in 1918

To fulfil this requirement of 20,000 men the Australian army set a minimum height requirement of 5ft 6inches. Preference was given to those men who had prior military experience

By the end of 1914, 52,561 had enlisted with many more thousands rejected on medical grounds

The increase in the number of engineers as a percentage of the British Army was much more modest compared to that of the Royal Artillery. The number of engineers rose from 5% to 7% of the entire army

Britain employed about 1,500 specialists within the gas warfare programme during the war

Between November 1916 and November 1917 the number of British motor vehicles in France doubled to just under 60,000

The British Army used men to carry messages to and from different parts of the line. These were called 'Runners' and were identified by red armbands around their left forearm

As well as carrying messages, runners were responsible for scouting the area before their battalion moved up to the front-line

The job of the Runner was very dangerous and they needed to be able to accurately read and interpret complicated trench maps

Signallers were responsible for sending messages using Morse code and telephone
In the early stages of the war, signallers laid telephone cables along the floor of the trenches. However these were continually broken by soldiers' boots so they started to dig them into the side walls of the trenches

Using the walls of the trenches for cables was an improvement but they still were vulnerable to artillery fire, so eventually all cables were laid underground

Signallers were trained in coding and de-coding messages as well as repairing and laying wires

As most of the repair work to cables had to be done during enemy artillery bombardments the casualty rates for signallers were very high

'Brass-hats' was the nickname given by the British Tommies to their high-ranking officers and generals

During 1918 the British military railway administration in France built or reconstructed 2,340 miles of broad-gauge and 1,348 miles of narrow-gauge railways

Britain also sent to France 1,200 locomotives and 52,600 rail cars to supplement existing French stock

'Suicide Ditch' was a term used by British soldiers to refer to the front-line trench

'Bantam' was a term to describe members of the army who were under the standard minimum accepted height of 5ft 3 inches

The front line infantry soldier was often disparaging to some of the support units, giving many of them nicknames – the Army Service Corps was known as the All Slackers Corps, the Army Veterinary Corps was known as All Very Cushy and the Royal Army Medical Corps were known as The Body Snatchers

Other regiments were not able to escape the wit of the average Tommy: The Royal Flying Corps was known as the Royal Flirting Corps, the Grenadier Guards was known as God's Gift and the Machine Gun Corps was known as Mother Goose's Children

PBI was an acronym used widely amongst the ranks of the British Army – it stood for 'Poor Bloody Infantry' and summed up the general feeling of those infantry soldiers that they were the last to be considered behind the artillery, cavalry engineers and other specialist units

A Town Major was a staff officer responsible for billeting arrangements in a town or village behind the lines

'Coffin Nails' was a term used by British soldiers to describe cigarettes

As Christmas 1914 approached, each British Tommy received plum puddings and a 'Princess Mary box', a metal case engraved with an outline of King George V's daughter and filled with chocolates, butterscotch, cigarettes and tobacco, a picture card of Princess Mary and a facsimile of George V's greeting to the troops, 'May God protect you and bring you safe home'

'Plugstreet' was British slang to describe the Belgian village of Ploegsteert

Men who joined the Territorial Force before the war were not obliged to serve overseas. However, when war was declared they were invited to do so and the majority did

90% of the East Lancashire Territorial Division did sign up for overseas service. They were men from men Blackburn, Bolton, Chorley and Burnley. By 10 September 1914 they had mobilised, moved to Southampton, and embarked for Egypt. They were the first British Territorials to go overseas as a complete formation

On 11 May 1915 the 1st Kite Balloon Section flew the first ever observation balloon near Steenvoorde in the Ypres sector of the Western Front

Lt O. Hogg and his gun team of No. 2 Anti-Aircraft Section of the Royal Garrison Artillery, led by Lt. I Hogg fired 75 rounds and shot down an enemy aircraft on 23 September 1914. It was the first time a German plane had been shot down by anti- aircraft fire

The first organised attack by British forces on the Western Front occurred on 13 October 1914 when infantry from 4th and 6th Divisions of Lt-Gen. Pulteney's III Corps attacked enemy positions on the Meterenbeek, near Hazebrouck

Men of the 18th (Service) Battalion, the Durham Light Infantry became the first men of Kitchener's New Armies to come under enemy fire. On 16 December 1914 they were shelled by the German warships *Derfflinger*, *Von Der Tann* and *Blucher*, whilst manning the trenches of the Tyne and Tees defences

At the outbreak of war, field gun batteries of the regular army had 6 guns, and those of the Territorial Force 4 guns. The standard weapons, which did not alter during the war other than by technical improvements, were the 18-lbr field gun, and the 4.5-inch howitzer

At full establishment, a brigade of British 18 pounder field guns consisted of 795 men of whom 23 were officers

Each 18 pounder gun had 1,000 rounds of ammunition within relative close proximity. A 4.5 inch Howitzer gun would have around 800 rounds per gun

If the fighting portion of a British Infantry Division was marching in approved formation down a road, it would be 8 miles in length

British infantry units marching on foot were expected to cover 98 yards in a minute. At that pace it would take 18 minutes to cover 1 mile

British wheeled transport in formation was expected to cover 2.5 miles in an hour, with motor lorries covering 6 miles in an hour

The Royal Engineers (RE) carried out a number of different roles for the army both in the battlefield and along the lines of communication

On 1 August 1914, the RE consisted of 1,056 officers and 10,394 men of the regular army and Special Reserve, plus another 513 and 13,127 respectively serving with the RE of the Territorial Force

In August 1917, the RE had grown to a total manpower of 295,668

In 1914, each infantry Division included two Field Companies. A third was added during January 1915. The Field Company was composed of 217 men

The Field Companies relied on horses for transport and had an establishment of 17 riding horses for the officers and NCOs of the Mounted Branch, plus 50 draught heavy horses, and 4 pack horses. There were also 5 spare draught horses as replacements

Field and Signal Companies were the most common of the RE units and provided the technical expertise at the front-lines

RE Survey units provided details of the battlefield on both sides of the wire, enabling infantry and artillery units to identify enemy positions and lay down accurate fire

'Special' Engineering Companies were formed in 1915 in retaliation of the German use of poison gas during the Second Battle of Ypres; these RE Special Companies were put in charge of Britain's own gas and chemical warfare tactics

As well as assisting above the ground, specialist Royal Engineer units called Tunnelling Companies were formed to take part in underground mining operations

The masses of men, kit, supplies, ammunition, weapons and rations were transported to the frontlines by railway, canal boats and ships. The Railway and Waterway Companies of the Royal Engineers maintained these vital transport links

In 1914 each infantry Division included a Signals Company with a total strength of 162 men

The Signals Companies relied on horses for transport and had an establishment of 33 riding horses plus 47 draught heavy and 4 pack horses. There were also 32 bicycles and 9 motorcycles

During the war, Haig suffered from toothache and sent for a Parisian dentist. Consequently, within months the army had hired a dozen dentists and by the end of the war there were 831 at the front, leading to the formation of the Royal Army Dental Corps in 1921

All British soldiers were issued with a jack-knife. This large folding knife had a blade, a spike and a rudimentary tin opener. To stop the soldiers losing their knives they were attached with a lanyard which was tied around the waist

When they signed up, each man was issued with a metal disc (later in the war a red fibre disc). On this disc was stamped his initials, surname, regimental number, regiment and religion

From September 1916 a second tag was added to ensure that if the wearer was killed one of the discs could be taken to help with identification.

When out of the line, the British Tommy would wear a soft trench cap. When not in use it was simply rolled up and stored in a soldier's haversack

The wearing of the trench cap became a matter of fashion and status: if it was worn flat and straight that would indicate a new soldier. Old sweats tended to wear their cap pulled back

The standard equipment worn by the average British Tommy made provision for 150 rounds of ammunition in ten pouches. Extra ammunition could be carried via a cotton bandolier

By 1917 every British unit had a 'salvage officer' who was responsible for the recovery of an kit that could be re-used, such as weapons, ammunition cases, empty tins, ration items, kits etc.

Cooks operating behind the line had to give over rabbit skins so they could be turned into gloves

Each battalion had a Medical Officer (MO) and a small team of medical personnel from the Royal Army Medical Corps. Their job was to look after the general health of the men of the unit

The British Tommy had many names for their German counterparts included 'Bosche' 'Jerry' Hun' and 'Fritz'

At the time of the war the average yearly wage for a skilled industrial worker was £75. Significantly lower than the income tax threshold of £160 per year

The Bull Ring was a large training ground for the British Army, there were many bull rings situated behind the lines. The largest one was in the town of Etaples

In Britain, many whisky distilleries were used to make explosives

All British newspapers received war news through the official Press Bureau and passed all the stories through the censors

Failure of the newspapers to follow official procedure on how to present the war news carried severe penalties under the Defence of the Realm Act. Punishment could include strict censorship and even closure of the newspaper

Canada had 3,100 regular ground troops in 1914

As war became imminent the Canadian government began to get together volunteers to form a Canadian Expeditionary Force (CEF)

Almost 600,000 Canadians enlisted to join the wartime army

418,000 Canadians served overseas with the CEF

12,000 Canadians were kept in Canada for home defence duties

The CEF suffered 210,000 casualties. 56,000 of these were killed

The CEF generally used British equipment although they did have Canadian built Ross rifles until 1916 when they were gradually replaced by the British Lee Enfield

Some 14,500 British nationals who were resident in Canada returned to Britain to enlist

In March 1915 the British government issued an appeal for women to join a Register of Women for War Service and by August 1916 some 750,000 women were employed in roles formally held by men

Another 350,000 women were working in jobs created specifically by the war (such as in munitions factories) and other 240,000 female agricultural workers made up the Land Army of spring 1918

After a demonstration by 300,000 women in London for the 'Right to Serve' the women's non-combatant armed forces were formed in 1917

9. COMBATANTS: GERMANY

The size of the German army in 1914 was around 840,000

Within one week of mobilisation, this 700,000 had been augmented by another 3.1 million men who had passed through 'universal service'

The German army mobilised about 13.8 million soldiers during the war

German troops fought not only on the Western Front, but also in Russia, the Balkans and Italy

German soldiers also fought alongside the Turkish army in Asia Minor and fought the Japanese in Eastern China, and served in Samoa, New Guinea and Africa

Stormtroopers comprised specially trained German assault troops used in 1918

For Christmas 1914 German soldiers at the front received a present from the Kaiser, the Kaiserliche, a large *meerschaum* pipe for the troops and a box of cigars for NCOs and officers

On reaching the age of 17, German males served in the 'Landsturm'

1st Battalion a group intended primarily for home defence. Every man belonged to the Landsturm 1st Battalion between the ages of 17-20, after which they commenced 2 years active service (or 3 years in the cavalry or horse artillery). After this each man served successive periods in the Reserve, Landwehr and finally the Landsturm 2nd Battalion when they reached 39 years old

During the war, a number of me aged between 17 and 20 years were allowed to volunteer for active service before their official call-up. These were known as Kreigsfreiwilligen (war volunteers)

Throughout the war, the German officer class continued to be sourced from the aristocratic and social elite. Despite the casualty rates, this structure was not relaxed

The German reserve of officers were made up of men from lower social groups and grew more than eight-fold during the war

A German infantry regiment consisted of three battalions. Each battalion was made up of 4 companies. There was also a separate machine gun company per regiment. In total there were around 64 officers and 3,203 men

German cavalry regiments consisted of four active squadrons and one depot squadron. With 724 active men (all ranks) per regiment

In 1914 Germany had 669 Infantry regiments. By January 1918 this had risen to 2,300. Similarly, artillery regiments rose from 1,042 in 1914 to 5,150 in January 1918

The German war machine had 2,000 scientists and technicians working within their gas warfare programme

8 of the German scientists who worked on their gas warfare project won the Nobel Peace Prize

During the war the Germans used 635,000 tons of barbed wire – it was enough wire to wrap around the circumference of the earth 130 times

During the war the Germans used 600 million sandbags

During the war the Germans used 160 million firework signals for communication from the front

Over 700,000 Belgian men were deported and forced to work in Germany

In August 1914, German troops shot and killed 150 civilians at Aerschot. The killing was part of war policy known as Schrecklichkeit (frightfulness). Its purpose was to terrify civilians in occupied areas so that they would not rebel

The artillery, (including foot, field, mountain, and horse artillery) was thought of as the elite section of the German Army

Peacetime German field artillery batteries consisted of six 7.7cm field guns. By 1915 all field batteries were reduced to 4 guns in order to preserve raw materials

By 1918 Field Howitzer Batteries formed almost one third of the total Field Artillery

The typical Field Artillery Battery contained 6 guns, 6 munitions wagons, 5 officers, 148 other ranks and 139 horses

German foot artillery contained the heavy guns. Prior to the breakout of war Germany possessed 400 batteries, by the end of the war this had grown to 2,250

In German Artillery speak, the term 'mortar' was used to describe any large howitzer of 21cm calibre and above

The typical Horse Artillery Battery consisted of 4 officers, 133 other ranks, 180 horses, 4 guns and 4 ammunition wagons

During the war Germany built up around 25 Mountain Artillery

Batteries. These were positioned along the front lines in the Balkans, the Alps, the Vosges and the Carpathian Mountains

A typical Mountain Battery boasted four 7.5cm quick firing guns that could be transported by mules. Some heavier mountain howitzers were also present in some Batteries

The regulation head gear in the early years of the war were the spiked helmets called the Pickelhaube

These Pickelhaube were worn with a field grey cover and usually bore the regimental number and letter: 'R' and number for reserve regiments, 'L' and number for Landwehr and an Iron Cross for the Landsturm

The Pickelhaube was gradually replaced with the distinctive Stahlhelm, coal scuttle steel helmet which was also used in various guises throughout WW2

The word Stahlhelm is German for steel helmet

In 1914 the German army possessed 782 field gun batteries, this rose to 1,691 by the end of the war

The average number of calories consumed each day by German adult civilians during January 1918 (the height of the naval blockade) was around 1,000

Paul von Hindenburg wrote 1,500 letters to his wife Gertrude during the war

By the end of 1916 the British naval blockade was having a serious effect on the German civilian population. Food was in such short supply than many people were suffering from extreme starvation

A German naval mutiny broke out on 28 October 1918. Officers were murdered as they defended their ships

On 12 March 1917 a Prussian War Ministry Order stated the strength of a typical infantry battalion should be 750 other ranks. This was a reduction in size due to the introduction of three light machine-gun units to each company

By 1918 the recommended strength of a Germany infantry battalion was about 850 other ranks without the machine guns

The Germans quickly realised that elite forward units, specifically trained for assault and trench raids could be very useful in trench warfare. Members were handpicked based on bravery and initiative and given specialist training away from the general infantry.

These assault companies were called Stosstruppe first used during the battle of Verdun

Stosstruppe proved so successful they were developed further until they were formed into official Sturmkompanies and attached to infantry divisions on a permanent basis

The average Sturmkompanie was made up of one officer and 120 other ranks

By 1918 these detachments had grown into battalions (Sturmbatallione) comprising 4 assault companies, an field gun battery, a light trench mortar battery, a machine gun company, a flame thrower unit and its own HQ set-up

These specialist detachments were the brainchild of Hauptmann Ulrich Rohr. He also designed much of the specialist equipment they used in the field

In 1918 there were 18 Sturmbattaliones known to be active

At the outbreak of war the German Army possessed 11 Cavalry Divisions. Each had 283 officers, 4,995 other ranks, 5,590 horses and 216 wagons

Attached to each Cavalry Division were 1 Jäger Battalion, 3 Batteries of Horse Artillery, 1 Cycle Company, a machine-gun unit, a Pioneer unit and a Signals unit

In 1914 every German Infantry Regiment included a machine gun company with 6 guns and a spare

As the benefits of the machine gun became more apparent, more and more new sections were formed, each consisting of 3 or 4 guns, 30-40 men and an officer

Special Machine Gun Marksman Sections were formed in early 1916 consisting of hand-picked gunners who had completed a special training course in using the machine gun in offensive situations

These elite machine gun units first saw action during the battle of Verdun and were attached to infantry regiments who were heavily involved in offensive operations or those who were in dangerous areas of the front line

There were roughly 200 Special Machine Gun Marksman Sections formed throughout the war

There were no specialist mining units in the German Army until 1916, by 1918 there were 50 such units each with about 4 officers and 250 other ranks when engaged in front line mining activities

'Gott Straffe England!' (God punish England!) was a German propaganda slogan, used on postage stamps, pin badges and other trinkets

10. COMBATANTS: RUSSIA

In 1911-12 it was estimated that the available male population within military age was more than 26 million

As the Russian army mobilised for the beginning of war in 1914 the Imperial Army stood at around 1,423,000 men

By the end of 1914 the Imperial Russian Army stood at over 6,500,000 men
In 1914 the Russian Army could only muster up about 4,000 Maxim machine guns

Regular army service was 3.5 years in the services from the age of 21, with another 14.5 years in reserve

Additional recruiting for the Russian army was via conscription, which had been in place since 1874

Conscription into the Russian army began at the age of 21 and continued through to the age of 43

Each reservist was requested to attend two 6-week training camps per year, however this could only really be enforced within the western geographical areas, due to travel requirements

In 1914 a Russian regiment consisted of 1,200 men. There were 117 Regiments as war was declared

41 of the 117 regiments were Cossack Regiments
The Cossacks were the Tsar's most reliable and able troops. They came from a long line of military tradition and were fiercely loyal to the Tsar

In 1914 some 939 Cossack units were mobilised, each unit contained roughly 100 men

Unfortunately the Cossacks only made up one fortieth of the total Russian manpower in the field

From 1909 Cossacks were allowed to carry ancient family weapons in place of regulation sabres

Cossacks served from the age of 20 until 38, doing 12 years in the field followed by 4 years each in the first, second and third category regiments before finishing up in the reserves

Cossacks had to provide his own uniform, equipment and horse. Only his rifle was supplied by the government

The sheepskin hat made famous by the Russian Cossaks was called a 'papakha'

During the war Russia mobilised over 12 million men, making it the largest army of the war

Tsar Nicholas II of Russia became Commander-in-Chief of the Russian Army on 5 September 1915

More than 75% of the Russian army were killed, wounded, or went missing in action

A Russian infantry company had only 2 NCOs. Compared to the average German company which usually had 12-16 NCOs

As the war progressed Russia struggled to produce enough weaponry and supplies for their front line troops. It was not uncommon for new recruits to arrive at the front un-armed. They would often use the weapons of fallen comrades

Russian manufacturing couldn't equip all of its soldiers with protective steel helmets

Drunkenness among the men was a perennial problem for the Russian army leaders

Despite advances in industrial manufacturing output and huge amounts of shells and guns bought in from overseas, supplies of weapons and ordnance at the front were in desperately short supply

Russia managed to improve production of 6 inch artillery shells from practically none in 1914, to 1.25 million in 1915 and on to a peak of 5.5 million in 1916. Despite this, their entire 1916 production would have only supplied the British guns for 2 or 3 weeks when engaged in heavy pre-bombardments such as those before the battle of the Somme

In the summer of 1916 the Russian II Corps was able to field an average of 11.4 field guns and 1.6 heavy artillery guns per mile across their front line. Compared to the French Sixth Army at the same time who boasted an average of 44.4 field guns and 64.5 heavy guns per mile across their section of the Western Front

The illiteracy rate amongst Russian soldiers was 75%. The highest out of all of the major combatants

Russian forces used the Zelinsky model 1916 gas mask. Shortages in manufacturing and logistical failures made distribution of this vital piece of equipment scarce to the front line soldier

No Muslims from Turkestan served in the Russian army because of distance, the language barrier and the fear of teaching them martial skills
Although Finns and Latvians did serve with the Russian army, the

authorities feared nationalism

Few Siberians served because of the extreme distance to conscript them

The Russians enjoyed success when they fought the Austro-Hungarian army simply because the staff work by the Austrian officers was very inefficient, especially when appraising Russian offensive capabilities

The average Russian soldier exhibited the same characteristics as their earlier ancestors: resolution, endurance and loyalty. However they were often let down by inept leadership, poor supply and inadequate levels of equipment and supplies

The production and sale of vodka was outlawed in Russia from August 1914

This law was not surprisingly unpopular and reduced the government's tax income by 30% practically overnight

At the beginning of the 20th century the Russian empire consisted of around 170 million people spread across almost 8 million square miles. All of this was ruled by just one man, the Tsar, Nicholas II

In an effort to counter the slow process of mobilising such a huge amount of men, most of the artillery budget from 1910-1914 was used in building up huge fortresses throughout Russian Poland in an effort to deter any would be aggressor

Germany was not the only country to have a pre-war plan. Like the Schlieffen Plan, Russia had her own strategy for a European war. 'Plan 19' was drawn up to counter the Austro-Hungarian and German threat to the east and the Turkish threat to the south. It used the Caucasus army to the south to deal with the Turks, with the main thrust of the Russian Army to be placed towards East Prussia

A revised Plan 19 was drawn up in May 1912 that reduced the forces moving into East Prussia and transferred them to face the slightly weaker Austria-Hungary Army

All Russian army groups were overseen by a supreme headquarters known as STAVKA

Half of the men that were called up each year were rejected/exempt on physical, personal or economic grounds

Russia had the largest working cavalry of all the warring nations in 1914
In 1914 a Russian infantry regiment, including regimental machine guns, engineers, communications and other specialist support troops, measured about 4,000 men

In 1914 the elite forces of the Russian Army were the Guards Corps. These were self-contained units and had their own engineers, artillery, communications and machine gun troops

It was the reserve battalions of the Guards stationed in Petrograd that provided the military muscle to the Revolution of 1917

By the end of 1915 the onset of trench warfare led to the raising of 'grenadier' units. The units were to carry out trench raids, gather intelligence on the enemy in the facing line of trenches and to carry out counter attacks
Men in the grenadier units were armed with hand grenades, swords and revolvers. The grenadier units were attached to ordinary line infantry regiments although to what extent is difficult to ascertain

Many Guards Corps units had centuries old traditions. The Pavlovski Guards Regiment was notable for recruiting only men with snub noses

At the outbreak of war the field army had only 240 heavy guns at their disposal. The majority of the artillery pieces were used to defend the fortresses along their huge frontier

St George's Battalions were not front line units but they were made up of hand-picked men who were highly decorated, and as such were seen as elite groups. Rank and file men needed to have been awarded the St George's Cross or Medal and the officers needed to have been awarded the Order of St George

In an attempt to shame the male soldiers into a more aggressive form of fighting, a number of Women's 'Battalions of Death' were raised in 1917. Only one battalion saw action though

11. COMBATANTS: FRANCE & BELGIUM

The French soldier was known as 'Poilus' which translates as 'The Bearded One'

This nickname was not universally liked by the French infantrymen; their traditional name was *'les biffins'* (rag and bone men)

In the trenches, the French infantry knew each other as *'les bon hommes'* (the lads) or as the war dragged on and the initial enthusiasm ebbed away, *'les pauvres cons du front'* or 'PCDF' (the poor bastards at the front)

The size of the peacetime French army in 1914 was approximately 820,000 – including 46,000 colonial troops

In the first 2 weeks of the war 2,887,000 reservists were called up and mobilised

A further 2,700,000 were mobilised by the end of June 1915

The pre-war French army was formed out of conscription, with every 20 year old male liable for 3 years' active service with the forces followed by 11 years in the reserves, 7 years in the Territorial Army and a final 7 years in the Territorial Reserve

Most French conscripts went into the infantry. There were strict limits on height and weight for entry into the cavalry, and preference was given to men with a background in telecommunications, railways and shipyards for entry into the engineers and the artillery

Most infantry conscripts were agricultural and manual workers, shop assistants and factory workers

French mobilisation was ordered on 1 August 1914

One the order for mobilization was given, the classes of 1896 to 1910 (men aged between 24 and 38) were called up immediately

Over 4,300 trains were used to get this first draft of men to their bases and training centres

In 1914 the French military machine 'acquired' more than 6,000 trucks, 2,500 cars, and over 1,000 omnibuses from civilian sources

During the war France mobilised approximately 8,500,000 men, of which 600,000 were colonials

In addition to these fighting troops, men were brought into France from abroad to work in industry and to serve in various works and labour units in the rear areas

Around 200,000 men from the French colonies, 100,000 foreigners (including 13,000 Chinese) and over 80,000 prisoners of war were also employed for various tasks

Non Commissioned Officers in the French Army were those who held the rank of sergeant. They were all promoted from the ranks

Promotion to the rank of Corporal or Sergeant was the sole decision of the Company Commander. Promotions further up, including to the ranks of sergeant-major and adjutant were made by the Colonel

For French soldiers there were 2 sets of rations depending on the current level of action the soldier was engaged in. Both rations included a base of 700g of bread, 300g of tinned meat and 600g of fresh meat along with 50cl of wine. Extra potatoes, pasta, sugar and coffee were also available

In French Muslim regiments, rations contained no pork and no alcohol

Every French regiment had a reserve stock of rations that was sufficient for several days

A small sum of money was available to each unit to spend on local produce if available, to supplement the army rations. This was normally looked after by the sergeant-major

Company mobile kitchens were normally situated in the second line of trenches, but often were even further behind the front lines. Food was carried to the front by working parties and was not an easy task especially during big battles

In September 1914 the French Army introduced a system of discipline and court marshalling where a sentence could be carried out within 24 hours without any right of appeal

Using this system the French Fourth Army was able to sentence 31 men to death in just 2 days in October 1914 for self-inflicted wounds. Out of these 31 men, 13 were actually shot

During the course of the war approximately 2,300 French soldiers were sentenced to death, although only 640 were actually shot

60% of all French executions took place before the end of 1915

25% of French soldiers from 1914 never returned home

The number of properly trained NCOs in the French Army was very low mainly due to the reduced conscription time of 2 years introduced in 1905. The Army didn't return back to 3 years until 1913

Another reason behind the lack of NCOs was that the best men with their mind set on an army career tended to become officers

French government policy was to try and ensure that 60% of officers were recruited from the ranks after a one year officer training course

At the outbreak of war, a French soldier's pay was 1 franc per day, with an extra franc per day earned as a 'trench allowance'

50 centimes of the trench allowance was withheld by the Army and used for an end of service gratuity which was delivered to the soldier upon demobilisation

During the war 155,000 Algerian and Tunisian soldiers were mobilised by France. 35,900 were killed

A French infantry division initially consisted of around 15,000 men, 36 field artillery guns and 24 machine-guns

There were 91 French cavalry Divisions at the outbreak of the war, each Division carried around 4,500 men

At the beginning of the war France boasted more than 106,000 mounted cavalrymen, but as the war progressed many cavalry units were disbanded with the men moved for service in the infantry. By the end of the war there were only 33,500 cavalrymen in service

The 4th RM (*régiments de marche* - equivalent to a British battalion) of the 1st Foreign Legion Regiment was known as the Garibaldi Brigade. It was made up almost entirely from Italian nationals and commanded by members of the Garibaldi family. It suffered so many casualties it was disbanded in 1915

The French Foreign Legion suffered so many casualties that by late 1915 all 16 regiments had been amalgamated into a single unit

The number of motorised vehicles in use by the French army at the front grew from some 19,000 in 1914 to over 88,000 in 1918

Artillery numbers grew steadily throughout the war. In early 1915 there were around 350,000 men manning the French artillery guns. By 1918 this had grown to over 600,000

The ratio between light and heavy artillery guns also changed significantly throughout the war. In 1914 heavy guns accounted for 8.3% of total French artillery, by 1918 heavy guns accounted for almost half of all French artillery pieces

After Captain Charles de Gaulle was captured at Verdun he attempted to escape from German POW camps 7 times

During the war there were around 17,000 separate French organisations making armaments

Margaretha Zelle (1876-1917), also known as Mata Hari, was a Dutch exotic dancer accused of being a double agent. Though she always denied being a spy, the French executed her in 1917

On 28 April 1917 a battalion of the French 18th Infantry Regiment refused to take their place in the front line. It was the first of many French mutinies that would happen over the next few weeks on the Western Front

The mutinies spread to 49 Infantry Divisions - 43% of the entire French Infantry

To stop the mutinies improvements were made in general living conditions, medical services and soldiers rest and leave time
23,000 soldiers were convicted of mutinous behaviour, with 554 sentenced to death

Only 27 French soldiers were executed for mutiny

4,278 trains were required to mobilise the French Army in August 1914

18% of the entire killed and missing casualty numbers inflicted on the French Army during the war occurred during the first 2 months of the war

These heavy losses can be part be accounted to their colourful uniforms, dating back to the 19th Century, that afforded the infantry little camouflage protection, as well as their peace-time training which concentrated on attacking in massed formations

It wasn't until mid-1915 that all troops were wearing the more restrained 'horizon blue' uniform which was more hardwearing and offered improved camouflage

The French army lost 2.7 men for ever German soldier casualty on the Western Front

By the end of 1915, 500,000 French soldiers had been reassigned to work in industry and manufacturing

The French 'Adrian' helmet issued in the summer of 1915 was the first tin hat issued in the war

By December 1915 more than 3 million Adrian helmets had been produced
Instead of a rum ration as per the British troops, the French Poilu had two rations of red country wine (called Pinard) a day

North African and other colonial French troops were given a khaki uniform described as 'mustard' after Christmas 1914

French soldiers were generally expected to move almost everywhere on foot. They were also required to carry with them clothing, bedding, food and drink (including their wine ration) equipment and ammunition

The combined weight of the kit a French soldier was expected to carry was approximately 40kg. The British Tommy carried around 30kg

French Poilus were notorious for their cavalier attitude to hygiene in the trenches. British troops hated taking over trench-lines formerly occupied by the French, and one of the first duties they usually undertook was to clean up the lines

By 1916, 50% of the pre-war French Army officer class had been killed

The number of infantry as a proportion of the overall French army decreased as the war progressed. There were more than 1.5 million infantrymen in service during the spring of 1915, by the Armistice there were only 850,000

In September 1914 the French army boasted 2,158 machine-guns. By 1918 there were more than 47,000 light machine guns and 19,000 heavy machine guns in front line service

The classes of 1892 to 1895 were called up in December 1914 and these were quickly followed by the classes of 1889 to 1891 who were called up in the spring of 1915

Each French cavalry division included a cycle battalion. During action the bicycle was folded in half and carried on the back of the rider

Units of the French Tenth Army, in the front line in the Ypres sector in April 1915 were the first men to be on the receiving end of gas attack. They had no defence against the gas and a complete enemy breakthrough was only negated at huge cost

The French made a few unsuccessful attempts to reduce sniper casualties with a variety of visors attached to the Adrian helmet. Almost all were difficult to manufacturer and proved of limited use in the field

The Belgian peacetime army amounted to one cavalry division and six infantry divisions. A total of around 43,000 men

Upon mobilisation in August 1914, the Belgian army was able to call up another 115,000 reservists

As well as the reservists there were also roughly 40,000 men in local reserve militia although these men were poorly trained and ill-equipped

Most Belgian officers were trained in France

More than a million Belgian refugees fled to the Netherlands, France and Great Britain in 1914

In the face of overwhelming superiority during the invasion of Germany, the Belgian army retreated to the fortified city of Antwerp. It was no use as Germany heavy artillery smashed Antwerp to pieces

By mid-December 1914 the Belgian army had been reduced to just over 32,000 men

Conscription from the small part of Belgium that remained free of German occupation enabled the Belgium Army to maintain an average strength of around 170,000 men

Due to the strict adherence of a neutral policy, the Belgians didn't take part in any Allied offensive. As a result the men were kept in decent condition and took an active part in the re-taking of Belgium land in the autumn of 1918

Small Belgian detachments did serve on loan to the Allies in many different areas on the Western Front and some colonial troops were active in East Africa

In total some 267,000 Belgians saw action during the war

54,000 Belgians were wounded with 14,000 killed

Belgium did not possess any naval forces at the time of the war

12. COMBATANTS: ANZAC

During the First World War soldiers from Australia and New Zealand were known as ANZACs

The joined forces were originally to be named the Australasian Army Corps but after complaints from the New Zealand forces it was changed to Australian and New Zealand Army Corps

Originally the term ANZAC was given to the cove on the Gallipoli peninsular where the Australians and New Zealanders landed in April 1915

Soon, the acronym was adopted by the soldiers that fought on the Gallipoli peninsular, but it later became a term associated with any Australian or New Zealand soldier who served in the First World War

Although synonymous with Australian and New Zealand troops, ANZAC was international in its makeup and at various points during the war contained units from India, Britain, the Pacific Islands and Sri Lanka

During the war Australian and New Zealand soldiers were known as 'Diggers' in the same way the British soldier was known as 'Tommy'

Before the war, New Zealand did not have a professional army; instead she relied on the Royal Navy and a local Territorial Force

The NZ Territorial Force of August 1914 had an effective fighting strength of 25,685

Due to the need for replacements of casualties, conscription was introduced to New Zealand on 16 August 1916

More than 100,000 New Zealanders answered the call to arms during the war, out of a just 243,376 available men of military age

The NZ conscription accounted for 10% of the entire population and 20% of the male population

The first New Zealand contingent to see overseas service in the war were the 1,400 men of the advance party of the New Zealand Expeditionary Force that sailed from Wellington on 12 August 1914 on route to German Samoa

A second contingent of NZ troops embarked from Wellington on 16 October 1914 bound for Britain, although they were re-routed to Egypt to help defend the Suez Canal from the Turks

Whilst in Egypt the NZEF was merged with the AIF to form the ANZAC

By the end of the war 550 nurses had served in the NZEF from Samoa to Gallipoli and on to the Western Front

New Zealand troops were the first Allied forced to capture and occupy German territory when 1,413 members of the NZEF landed unopposed at Apia in German Samoa on 29 August 1914

Around 3,100 New Zealanders landed at ANZAC Cove, Gallipoli on the first day of landings. Over 600 became casualties

During the war New Zealand forces suffered 59,483 casualties and 18,166 of these were killed

In November 1917, AIF orders authorised the wearing of a small badge in the form of the letter 'A' on the shoulder of a soldier's uniform to denote that the wearer had taken part in the 1915 Gallipoli campaign

Nurses who worked on hospital ships anchored off the peninsular and hospitals on nearby islands were also eligible to wear this 'A' badge

Some ANZAC soldiers also wore ANZAC rosettes. These were issued to men who had enlisted very early in 1914 and came home early on "ANZAC Leave" from mid-1918. The rosette was worn so that apparently able-bodied men would not be accused of shirking their duty

Following the evacuation from the Peninsular the ANZAC were split into two new formations: I ANZAC Corps and II ANZAC Corps

ANZAC Day (25th April) commemorates the first day of the Gallipoli Landings in 1915

More than 11,000 ANZACs died on the Gallipoli Peninsula, despite only being there for 8 months

The original ANZAC biscuit was known as an ANZAC wafer or tile and was part of the rations given to ANZAC soldiers during World War I. They were included instead of bread because they had a much longer shelf life

Australian infantry forces were organised solely for home defence before 1914

The Australian army was formed in 1901

In 1913 the Australian Army was just 2,235 strong with another 21,461 men serving in the militia

On 3 August 1914 the Australian government offered to help Britain by providing 20,000 troops for the war effort

Because existing militia forces were unable to serve overseas, an all-volunteer expeditionary force, the Australian Imperial Force (AIF) was formed from 15 August 1914

The Australian government was very concerned about the German colonies of Samoa and New Guinea, situated to the north of Australia. Although the garrisons were small on these islands, the posed a threat to Australian shipping

To deal with this more local threat the Australian Naval and Military Expeditionary Force (AN&MEF) enlisted 2,000 men independently of the AIF

The Imperial Camel Corp was created in January 1916 from four Australian camel companies to quash the threat from the German sponsored Arab religious movement, the Senussi

By the end of 1916 the Camel Corps was expanded to total ten Australian camel companies, two New Zealand companies and six British companies

By the end of the war, almost 20% of those who served in the Australian forces had been born in the United Kingdom, even though nearly all enlistments had occurred in Australia

As part of the recruitment drive, posters and leaflets promised an opportunity to see England and Europe

Australian troops were paid a minimum of 6 shillings a day which was more than 3 times the pay of the average British Private. This led to the phrase '6 bob a day tourists' coined by the British

6 shillings per day was slightly under minimum wage in Australia but due to high unemployment and tough financial conditions this kind of money was still attractive to many

By July 1915 the minimum height requirement had fallen to 5ft 2 inches and the age limit had risen from 38 until 45 as new men were needed to replace Gallipoli casualties

The first AIF and New Zealand troopship set sail for Egypt (for training) on 7 November 1914

416,809 Australians enlisted for service in the First World War, representing 38.7% of the total male population aged between 18 and 44

331,781 Australians served overseas during the war, suffering almost 210,000 casualties

At almost 65%, the Australian casualty rate (proportionate to total embarkations) was the highest of the war

Only 4,000 Australians became Prisoners of War

Private William Edward 'Billy' Sing of the 5th Australian Light Horse successfully sniped at least 150 Turkish soldiers whilst serving at Gallipoli. As a result he was giving the nickname 'The Murderer'

Private Sing was awarded the Distinguished Conduct Medal for his sniping skills

63 Australians were awarded the Victoria Cross during the War

The last surviving ANZAC, Alec Campbell, died on May 16, 2002

Private John 'Barney' Hines of the 45th Btn. Australian Infantry, was obsessed with souvenir collecting and would comb the battlefields for watches, badges, weapons and enemy uniform. His souveniring became legendary at the front and included a piano and a grandfather clock that he managed to get into the trenches until his fellow Australians blew it to pieces with grenades to stop the hourly chiming that attracted the unwanted attention of the enemy

James Charles Martin (3 January 1901 – 25 October 1915) was the youngest Australian known to have died in World War I. He was only 14 years and 9 months old when he succumbed to typhoid during the Gallipoli campaign

JC Martin was one of 20 Australian soldiers under the age of 18 known to have died in World War I.

During summer 1918 Australian front line troops took part in numerous trench raids as they pushed the German Army back. The Diggers called this 'ratting' or 'prospecting'

Often during such 'ratting' violent hand-to-hand fighting broke out and the Diggers loaded up on specialist close quarter weapons such as trench knives, knuckledusters, improvised axes and bayonets

The most successful raid of this type occurred on 11 July 1918 when men of the Australian 1st Division captured 1,000 yards of enemy front line, capturing 120 German prisoners and 11 machine guns in the process

During this chapter of the war, General Sir Herbert Plumer, commander of the British Second Army, commented that 'there is no division, certainly in my army, perhaps in the whole British army, which has done more to destroy the morale of the enemy than the 1st Australian Division'.

In 1919 more than 150 Australian soldiers volunteered to serve alongside the British Army during the Allied intervention of the Russian civil war

The Australian Army Nursing Service provided 2,139 nurses for overseas service during the war. They were attached to both Australian and British medical units

13. COMBATANTS: UNITED STATES OF AMERICA

In 1914 the size of the US Army was 126,000 men, with another 81,000 reservists that could be called upon if required

On 18 May 1917 Congress passed the Selective Service Act requiring all male citizens between the ages of 21 and 31 to register for the draft

5 June 1917 was declared National Draft Day and was set for initial registration of men between the ages of 21 and 31

On this first National Draft Day around 10 million young American men registered for Selective Service

The average American soldier stood 5ft 7inches tall and weighed 145 pounds

Each man that enrolled received their draft card which proved they had enrolled and that they weren't a 'slacker'

Conscripts made up 72% of the US Army during WW1

Prior to the war it was US Army standard policy for each new recruit to undergo 12 months of training before being considered for combat

This 12 months soldier training would typically consist of 6 months of garrison training and 6 months field instruction.

The trainers for the new recruits were typically NCOs of the new recruit's future unit

Roughly 25% of the US Army during the war was foreign born. Many of these men had emigrated to America as teenagers or adults and as a result knew very little English

To cope with the large numbers of non-English speaking recruits, a Foreign Speaking Soldier Subsection (FSS) was established to help train this group of men

In addition to the basic training, the FSS soldiers also received 3 hours of English lessons per day

In preparation for the First World War, the new theory was that all new recruits would get 3 months training although the soldiers of the FSS received 4 months

In order to prepare for trench warfare, mock trenches were dug in many of the training camps that sprouted right across America

In order to help the US Army understand the nature of warfare on the Western Front many British and French officers were brought over to help train the troops and brief the commanders

Due to a shortage of weapons wooden rifles were often used for drill and training

The American Expeditionary Force was controlled by Major General John J. Pershing. The troops gave him the nickname of 'Black Jack'

General Pershing wanted his army to be skilled in the art of open warfare and as a result a lot of time and effort was dedicated to a war of movement and offensives

Pershing insisted that all AEF units be larger in formation than normal. He wanted this for two main reasons; he recognized that large casualties would be a formality and wanted his army units to be able to cope with this, also fewer separate units would conceal the fact he had a severe lack of trained officers

A typical AEF infantry battalion consisted of a commander, 26 officers and 1,027 men. An infantry brigade was made up of 6 battalions plus a machine gun battalion and various support functions. It had a strength of about 8,400 men and was similar in size and strength to a British infantry Division

A US Infantry Division was made up of four battalions, roughly 28,000 men and included artillery, signals, engineers and machine gun units

Although there was no official segregation policy within the draft, African Americans were asked to rip off the corner of their draft applications so they could be easily identified

The primary infantry weapon at the start of the war was the 1903 Model Springfield rifle

At the beginning of the war only 600,000 1903 rifles were available

By June 1917 14,000 US Soldiers had already arrived in France

The US infantry did not see front line action until late October 1917 when the US 1st Division entered trenches near Nancy

By May 1918 over 1,000,000 US Soldiers were stationed in France, with half of them seeing front line action

American troops also helped to build up French infrastructure to carry increased men, supplies and weapons to the front lines. American engineers in France built 82 new ship berths, nearly 1,000 miles of standard gauge railway tracks and 100,000 miles of telephone and telegraph lines

By the end of the war the USA had mobilised 4,355,000 men

Almost 2,000,000 American troops crossed the North Atlantic from 1917-18

In order to get as many men to the front as quickly as possible the AEF left many of its heavy guns behind and had to rely on British and French weaponry

At the time of the First World War African Americans could not serve in the US Marine Corps and could only hold lowly and menial positions in the US Navy and the US Coast Guard

At the beginning of the war, the US Army had four Divisions specifically for African Americans: the 9th and 10th Cavalry and the 24th and 25th Infantry; however these were not involved in any overseas combat action. Instead they were deployed in American held territories

More than 200,000 African Americans served in WWI, but only about 11% of them saw combat. The majority worked in labour units, loading cargo, building roads, and digging trenches.

After protests from the African American community that they were not being allowed to fight the US government created the 92nd and 93rd Infantry Divisions in 1917

To this day the insignia of the United States 93rd Infantry Division is a blue French Adrian helmet against a black background, due to the fact they were sent to the front line to fight alongside the French without the required equipment, and were force to wear the French Adrian helmet

With the creation of these new Divisions it was decided that it would be better if these would be led by African American officers. In May 1917 a segregated officer camp was set up in Des Moines, Iowa

When the doors to the camp opened, 1,250 men enrolled in officer training for the new Divisions

On 15 October 1917, 639 African American men received their commissions and were assigned to officer positions in the infantry artillery and engineers. It was to be the first and last commissions issued at Des Moines as it was shut down soon afterwards

The 92nd Infantry Division suffered from huge negative press within the US Army with even their own (racist) senior officers exaggerating negative stories to give them a bad name

Each US Infantry regiment had a heavy weapons unit which operated 16 heavy machine guns, 4 37mm guns and 6 mortars

The machine guns used by the US Army were meant to be US manufactured Brownings, however due to production and supply issues many units used French Hotchkiss guns instead

Only 57,000 Browning machine guns were produced before the end of the war

Each American Infantry Division could boast 224 heavy machine guns, compared with around 100 guns for a German Infantry Division

The 369th Infantry Regiment was the first unit from the 93rd Division to reach France, arriving in December 1917. In March 1918 they were pushed into the fighting around the Argonne Forest where they quickly earned the nickname the 'Harlem Hellfighters'

From 26 September to 5 October 1918 the 369th Infantry Regiment took part in the Muesse-Argonne offensive where they fought in the front line for a total of 191 days. France awarded the entire unit the Croix de Guerre

Very few African Americans saw combat action during the war, the vast majority were forced to work in service and labour regiments

By the end of the war African Americans served in cavalry, infantry, signal, medical, engineer and artillery units

Some Americans disagreed with the United States' initial refusal to enter WWI and so they joined the French Foreign Legion or the British or Canadian army. A group of US pilots formed the Lafayette Escadrille, which was part of the French air force and became one of the top fighting units on the Western Front.

Woodrow Wilson's campaign slogan for his second term was, 'He kept us out of war.' About a month after he took office, the United States declared war on Germany on April 6 1917

As soon as the declaration or war was issued volunteers flocked to recruiting offices to sign up. Volunteers had to be a minimum of 18 years of age and have at least twenty teeth

To increase the size of the US Army during WWI, Congress passed the Selective Service Act, which was also known as the conscription or draft, in May 1917

During WWI, people of German heritage were suspect in the US. Some protests against Germans were violent, including the burning of German books, the killing of German shepherd dogs, and even the murder of one German-American.

Herbert Hoover, who would become president in 1929, was appointed US Food Administrator. His job was to provide food to the US army and its allies. He encouraged people to plant 'Victory Gardens', or personal gardens. More than 20 million Americans planted their own gardens, and food consumption in the US decreased by 15%

During US involvement in WWI, more than 75,000 people gave about 7.5 million 4-minute pro-war speeches in movie theatres and elsewhere to about 314.5 million people

'Hello Girls,' as American soldiers called them, were American women who served as telephone operators for Pershing's forces in Europe

All 'Hello Girls' were aged between 18 and 35 and were fluent in French. They were all specially trained by the American Telephone and Telegraph Company

Even though the US government didn't grant Native Americans citizenship until 1924, nearly 13,000 of them served in WWI

The American Expeditionary Force (AEF) was forced to rely on French and British artillery; specifically the French 75mm field gun and the 155mm howitzer

The 1st US Light Tank Brigade, commanded by George S. Patton, was made up entirely of Renault FT tanks

By October 1918 there were 120 American Infantry regiments in action on the Western Front

During the battle of Belleau Wood in June 1918 the US Army suffered 5,200 casualties per square mile

At the time of the Armistice, US forces were holding 23% of the Allied line on the Western Front

The American Infantry were affectionately known as 'doughboys', although from 1917 this term was used to describe all aspects of the American armed forces

American soldiers were also known as 'Yanks' or 'Sammies' (from 'Uncle Sam')

The last surviving 'Doughboy' was Frank Buckles who drove Army Ambulances in France in 1918. He died in February 2011 aged 110

An American Infantry Private (First Class) was paid $30 per month. A Regimental Sergeant Major was paid $51 per month

Corporal Freddie Stowers was the only African-American to receive the Congressional Medal of Honor in World War I

'Devil Dogs' was the nickname given to the US Marines by the German Army

The US M1917 steel helmet was a close replica of the British helmet with some slight differences in the inner liner and strap

When the American troops started to land in France the cost for a quart of champagne was 70 cents and for a fifth of cognac it was $1. These prices quickly rose to $5 a quart of champagne and $10 for a fifth of cognac as soon as French retailers figured out the extent of the American pay packet

Whilst undergoing training in France, most of the US Army lived in small towns and villages. Churches, barns and granaries were converted into makeshift barracks. These buildings were damp, cold and riddled with lice and rats

In 1916 an officers' training summer camp was set up in Plattsburg, New York. It was the first of many Officer Training Camps that were to spring into life across the nation. These OTCs produced huge numbers of college educated junior officers

These new officers were nicknamed '90 day wonders' but made up almost 50% of the entire US Army's officer requirements. A further 10% were promoted directly from the rank and file

The US Army Nurse Corps (ANC) had over 5,000 nurses serving at the front in July 1918

US nurses were paid around $60 a month and were given many of the same courtesies as infantry officers

By the Armistice there were 10,000 American nurses on active service, most of whom were assigned to hospital trains and convalescent wards

175,000 men were employed in trying to supply the AEF with enough vehicles, guns, ammunitions, animals, weapons and other supplies

During the war, the US shipped about 7.5 million tons of supplies to France to support the Allied effort. That included 70,000 horses or mules as well as nearly 50,000 trucks, 27,000 freight cars, and 1,800 locomotives

During WWI, American hamburgers (named after the German city of Hamburg) were renamed Salisbury steak. Frankfurters, which were named after Frankfurt, Germany, were called 'liberty sausages', Sauerkraut was renamed 'victory cabbage' and dachshunds became 'liberty dogs'

US schools also stopped teaching German

13. COMBATANTS: ITALY

The Italian Government introduced military conscription in 1907. However, only about 25% of those eligible for conscription received training

By 1912 there were 300,000 in the Italian Army but there was a shortage of experienced NCOs and trained officers.

In 1914 the Italian army had only 13,000 serving officers and suffered throughout the war with a shortage of leaders in the field

The shortages of manpower were so severe that some companies that should have had a mobilised strength of around 250 men could only muster 15. There were hardly any NCOs and many reserve officers had no front line experience

King Vittorio-Emanuele was technically the Italian Commander-in-Chief and spent the war close to the front, but in reality the army was run by General Cadorna, the Italian Chief of General Staff

In July 1914 General Luigi Cadorna became chief of staff of the Italian Army

In August 1914 Italy declared herself neutral, despite being part of the Triple Alliance with Germany and Austria-Hungary

As soon as war was declared mobilisation kicked in at a rapid pace and continued throughout the entire war. At the time of the Armistice the army was 5.2 million strong

In secret talks, officially known as the Treaty of London, Italy joined forces with the Triple Entente of Russia, France and Britain in return for significant territorial gains if they were victorious in the war

Italy signed the Treaty of London on 26 April 1915

On 3 May 1915 Italy officially revoked the Triple Alliance

Official mobilisation of the Italian army occurred on 22 May 1915

Italy declared war on Austria-Hungary on 23 May 1915

On 28 August 1916 Italy declared war on Germany

On 26 May Italy commenced a naval blockade of Austria-Hungary

The pact was to be kept secret, but after the October Revolution in 1917 in Russia, it was published by the Russian journal Izvestia

The Treaty of London was nullified by the Treaty of Versailles

In his Fourteen Points, US President Woodrow Wilson contained a number of clauses that were against the provisions of the Treaty of London, as a result many of Italy's territorial claims were cancelled

In the spring of 1915 the Italian army stood at 25 infantry and 4 cavalry divisions

The Italian army of early 1915 only had 120 heavy or medium artillery pieces and only around 700 machine guns in total

Between 1915 and 1918 the Italian army launched eleven separate offensives on the Isonzo River

Approximately 275,000 Italian prisoners were taken during the Caporetto offensive – a spectacular Austro-German success on the Italian front

The main effort of the Italian forces was in the Isonzo and Vipava valleys. As on the Western Front the campaign quickly turned to static trench warfare, however instead of mud the trenches had to be dug into the sides of Alpine slopes and glaciers, often up to 3,000m (9,800 ft) above sea level

On 3 November 3, Italian troops entered the city of Trento (Trent) and captured 300,000 Austrian soldiers, including the philosopher Ludwig Wittgenstein

Fighting ended on the Italian Front on 4th November 1918

The frequency of offensives for which the Italian soldiers partook between May 1915 and August 1917 was practically one every three months. This rate was higher than demanded by the armies on the Western Front

Italian discipline was significantly harsher than other armies, with relatively minor offenses punishable by severe repercussions

Due to heavy losses sustained in the war, by summer 1918 the Italian Government were forced to call up the so-called 99 Boys (Ragazzi del '99), that is, all males who were 18 years old

The Italian army had something of a poor reputation during the war. Rommel once said that one Württemberg alpine soldier was worth 20 Italians

570,000 Italians were invalided out of service due to wounds

At full strength an Italian infantry battalion was 1,043 strong

Early in the war each regiment formed their own 'death companies' to lead offensives, cut enemy wire etc. These soldiers would wear body armour that looked like a medieval suit of armour

By 1917 these death companies had morphed into elite assault groups that were heavily armed with machine guns, flame throwers, grenades and daggers

In 1914 the Italian field artillery was 289 batteries strong, with each battery containing four guns. By the Armistice this had risen to 490 batteries

Italian heavy artillery was very weak in 1914 with just 30 4-gun batteries in existence in 1914. By 1918 this had grown to 280 batteries

The Italians were the first to use airplanes in war, in Libya from October 1912

Under the recruitment scheme of 1907, all able bodied Italian men between the ages of 19 and 38 years old were liable for call up to the army

By May 1915 Italy had mobilized 23,039 officers, 852,217 other ranks and 9,163 civilians

During the war the Italian army expanded massively, with 181 new combat battalions had been added by the end of 1915

By the end of the war 5.2 million Italian men were serving

A high level of illiteracy in the ranks of the Italian infantry meant that not enough men were able to be promoted to become NCOs

Large differences in dialects made communication difficult with some groups, such as those from Sardinia, being almost impossible to understand by others

The Italian infantry rank and file was poorly paid in comparison to others in Europe. Home leave was rare, rations were inadequate and front line facilities were truly substandard. Despite this, morale at the front was generally not a problem

General Cadorna was a strict disciplinarian and not afraid of removing people who went against him in less than 3 years he dismissed some 800 senior officers

Cadorna himself was sacked after the defeat at Caporetto and a reorganization of the army shortly afterwards resulted in better wages for the front line troops as well as better rations, more leave and even free life insurance to ensure their families were looked after if they were killed in action

The 'Arditi' (bold ones) were hand-picked soldiers who formed specialist assault group. They formed heavily armoured groups and became an inspiration for the rest of the infantry due to their bravery, daring and also their apparent disregard for authority

At the beginning of the war the Italian artillery possessed only 112 heavy guns

Italy only had sufficient stocks of artillery shells to cope with a short war and thus was severely hit by a shortage of shells. Production steadily improved and more shells were brought in from France and Britain to make up the short fall

Generally the Italian trenches were not as well constructed as their Austro-Hungarian counterparts, mainly because they were on the offensive for most of the time and they didn't expect to spend much time and effort building strong defensive lines

14. BRAVERY

634 Victoria Crosses were awarded during WW1

Captain Noel Chavasse (RAMC) was the only man awarded the Victoria Cross twice during the war

The first Canadian winner of the Victoria Cross during the war was Lance Corporal Frederick Fisher who won his VC on 23 April 1915 at St Julien, France

During an offensive patrol over Mansue, Italy on 30 March 1918 the Sopwith Camel of Lt. Alan Jerrard was hit 163 times by enemy fire. Jerrard was awarded the Victoria Cross

The average age of WW1 Victoria Cross winners was 27.5 years

The number of Victoria Crosses awarded by year:
- 1914 - 46 awards
- 1915 - 117 awards
- 1916 - 84 awards
- 1917 - 175 awards
- 1918 - 207 awards

30 recipients of the Victoria Cross during the war were teenagers

4 recipients of the Victoria Cross during the war were in their 50's

The first Indian winner of the Victoria Cross during WW1 was Sepoy Khudadad Khan who won his VC at Hollebeke, Belgium on 31 October 1914

Of all of the winners of the Victoria Cross during the war, 166 were killed or died of wounds received during their VC action

2nd Lt William Rhodes-Moorhouse won the first VC to the Royal Flying Corps on 26 April 1915

The oldest recipient of the VC during the war was Marine Master Fred Parslow. He was 59 years old

3 men from one street in Canada (Pine Steet, Winnipeg) were all awarded the VC; CSM Frederick Hall, Corporal Leo Clarke and Lt. Robert Shankland. Their street was named 'Valour Road' in their honour

The youngest recipient of the Victoria Cross was Boy (First Class) John Cornwell. He served on HMS Chester and was 16 years old

The number of Victoria Crosses awarded by country:
- Britain and Ireland - 475
- Australia - 60
- Canada - 60
- India - 18
- New Zealand - 11
- South Africa - 3

There were 1,116 Distinguished Flying Crosses (DFC) awarded during WW1. This award was bestowed for 'acts of valour, courage or devotion to duty performed whilst flying in active operations'

Subsequent awards for the DFC were recognised by a silver slide on bar added to the original medal ribbon. 75 Airmen received the Bar to the DFC

Three airmen were awarded 2 Bars to the DFC:

- Captain Arthur Henry Cobby (Australia - 29 kills)
- Captain Walter Hunt Longton (Britain - 11 kills)
- Captain Ross MacPherson Smith (Australia - 12 kills)

Captain W.H. Longton's medal group was sold at auction for £36,000 in December 2011

On 22 December 1915 Second Lieutenant Alfred Victor Smith, of the 1/5th Battalion, the East Lancashire Regiment (T.F.) was throwing a grenade, when it slipped from his hand and fell to the bottom of the trench rolling close to several British officers and men. He shouted, and he jumped clear, but seeing that the others could not get into cover, he turned and flung himself down on to the grenade. The explosion instantly killed him. He was posthumously awarded the Victoria Cross

The Distinguished Service Order (DSO) was the second highest decoration available to the British Army. It was awarded mainly to senior officers (rank of Major and above)

8,981 Distinguished Service Orders were awarded during WW1

3,758 DSOs were awarded to officers of the British Army

Of those 3,758 awards 446 were awarded for gallantry, 582 were awarded for distinguished service, 180 for meritorious service and 2,550 for combat command

Multiple DSO awards were denoted by gilt bars ornamented by a crown
- 720 Bars to the DSO were awarded during the war
- 75 Second Bars to the DSO were awarded during the war
- 7 Third Bars to the DSO were awarded

37,081 Military Crosses were awarded during the war

The Military Cross was awarded for acts of gallantry carried out by junior officers that did not qualify for the VC or DSO

For multiple awards, recipients were given a silver bar ornamented by a crown

There were 2,995 Bars to the Military Cross awarded during the war

There were 188 2nd Bars to the Military Cross awarded during the war

There were 4 3rd Bars to the Military Cross awarded during the war

Company Sergeant Major John (Jack) Henry Williams VC, DCM, MM & Bar, is the most decorated Welsh non-commissioned officer of all time

In February 1919 CSM Williams received the Victoria Cross, Distinguished Conduct Medal, and the Military and Bar from King George V. It was the first time that the King had decorated the same man four times in one day

On 28 June 1919 Lt Colonel Percy Hone, Middlesex Regiment (attached Durham Light Infantry) was awarded the Distinguished Service Order and Bar, and the Military Cross and two Bars at the same time from the King. Five awards at once.

The highest award for bravery issued by the American Armed forces was the Congressional Medal of Honor. The recipients' act of bravery had to be witnessed and recommended first hand by an officer

119 Americans were awarded the Congressional Medal of Honor during the war

Out of the 119 awards of the Congressional Medal of Honor, 33 were awarded posthumously. Translating to 27.7% of all awards

During the war there were two versions of the Congressional Medal of Honor; one for the navy and one for the army

Gunnery Sergeant Robert Guy Robinson was shot 13 times during a dogfight over Belgium on 14 October 1918. Despite this he fought off 12 enemy machines and returned to base. He was awarded the Congressional Medal of Honor for his troubles

Sergeant Alvin C York became one of the most decorated American soldiers of the war. He won the Congressional Medal of Honor on 8 October 1918 when he led an attack on a German machine gun nest during the Meuse-Argonne offensive. He captured 32 machine guns, killed 28 enemy and took 132 prisoners, practically single-handedly

On 12 August 1918 HM King George V knighted Lt General John Monash, commander of 3rd Australian Division, on the battlefield in recognition of his outstanding leadership. The first such decoration in the field for over 200 years

Captain 'Mad Harry' Murray (13th Australian Battalion) was awarded the DCM at Gallipoli, the DSO for gallant leadership at Mouquet Farm in August 1916, the Victoria Cross for leading his unit in the capture of Stormy Trench at Gueudecourt in February 1917 and a bar to his DSO for gallantry at Bullecourt in April 1917

One of the most iconic awards for bravery is the Iron Cross. During the First World War there were three grades of this award. The Iron Cross 2nd Class, the Iron Cross 1st Class and the Grand Cross of the Iron Cross

The Iron Cross 2nd Class was a traditional medal, with a ribbon, whereas the 1st Class award was a pin badge worn on the breast pocket

Both the 2nd and 1st classes of Iron Cross were awarded regardless of rank

The Grand Cross of the Iron Cross was awarded only to high ranking officers and officials

One had to already possess the Iron Cross 2nd Class in order to receive the 1st Class award

Around 5,196,000 Iron Cross 2nd Class medals were awarded

Approximately 218,000 Iron Cross 1st Class awards were issued

There were only 5 awards of the Grand Cross of the Iron Cross made during the First World War

The 5 recipients of the Grand Cross of the Iron Cross were: Kaiser Wilhelm II, Paul von Hindenburg, Erich Ludendorff, Prince Leopold of Bavaria and August von Mackensen

The Star of the Grand Cross of the Iron Cross was the highest award of the German Empire and was awarded to the most outstanding of generals who performed feats of leadership to the extreme benefit of the German state. It was awarded only twice in history

Paul von Hindenburg's award of the Grand Cross of the Iron Cross was upgraded to the Star of the Grand Cross of the Iron Cross in March 1918. This was the only the second time in history this award had been bestowed, and it would be the final time

Known informally as 'The Blue Max' the Pour le Mérite was the highest order of merit issued by the Kingdom of Prussia

Instituted in 1740 by King Frederick II of Prussia, it has a French name because that was the leading language of the Prussian court at that time

There were 687 Pour le Mérite awards bestowed during the war. 533 were awarded to the army

There were 20 foreign awards of the Pour le Mérite: 14 went to members of the Austrian-Hungarian forces, 4 to Bulgarian forces and 2 to Turkish forces

There were 29 U-boat officers decorated with the Pour le Mérit

The first Pour le Mérite to be awarded during the war was bestowed on General von Emmich on 7 August 1914. It was awarded in honour of his leadership role in the battle to neutralise the Liege fortifications

The last order conferred was to flying ace Theo Osterkamp on 2 September 1918

For airmen to be awarded the Blue Max they had to shoot down 8 enemy aircraft. This was increased to 16 by early 1917 and up to 30 by the end of the war

A second award resulted in a spray of gilt oak leaves attached above the cross. But these were usually reserved for high ranking officers only

There were 122 oak leaves awarded during WW1

The Order could not be awarded posthumously. Many awards had to be cancelled because the would-be recipient died whilst the paperwork was being drawn up

France introduced the Croix de Guerre on 8 April 1915 as a reward for distinguished service at the front

The ribbon of the Croix de Guerre bore different stars or palm leaves depending on the award; a bronze star was awarded for a mention in regimental or brigade orders, a silver star for divisional orders, a gilt star for corps orders or a bronze palm leaf for army orders

Five bronze stars were exchanged for a silver palm leaf

Awards of the Croix de Guerre could also be awarded to entire regiments in the form of a lanyard made out in the colours of the medal ribbon

During the action that won him the Military Cross, Siegfried Sassoon was shot by a sniper and was moved to a casualty clearing station that was run by Medical Officer William Kelsey Fry. Sassoon was notified whilst at the CSS that he had been awarded the Military Cross but he was slightly disappointed that he had to wait to receive the actual decoration. William Kelsey Fry unpicked his own MC ribbon from his tunic, won at Festubert, and sewed it on to Sassoon's uniform

During an American advance in the Battle of Belleau Wood, the first waves of marines were either killed or dead or pinned to the ground, scared to move. Two-time Congressional Medal of Honor winner Gunnery Sergeant Dan Daly, suddenly jumped up with his rifle high in the air and screamed to his fellow Marines, 'Come on you sons of bitches! Do you want to live forever?' He then charged full-tilt towards the woods. An attack that was once floundering was now gathering a new momentum. By the end of the day the Marines had a small foothold in the woods. For his actions that day Daly won the Navy Cross and the French Croix de Guerre

On 29 September 1918 Lt Frank Luke was the leading American air 'Ace'. He was shot down over enemy lines whilst having a pistol fight. He was posthumously awarded the Medal of Honor

15. ANIMALS

Horses were used for pulling artillery, wagons and ambulances as well as reconnaissance work

On just one day during the Battle of Verdun in 1916 7,000 horses were killed by shelling

8 million horses died on all sides during the war

Another 2.5 million horses were treated in veterinary hospitals for wounds and illness

Britain and Commonwealth forces lost 484,143 horses during the war

Only 62,000 horses returned home to Britain after the war

At any given time the German army had some 1.5 million horses and mules working at the front line

Approximate German horse casualties are 400,000 killed due to enemy fire and another 500,000 due to sickness and disease

Sergeant Stubby, a Boston Bull Terrier, was the most decorated dog of the war and the only dog to be promoted to the rank of sergeant

Sergeant Stubby served on the Western Front for 18 months with the US 106th Infantry and took part in 17 battles

Because Stubby could hear the whine of artillery shells before humans he was very useful in warning his regiment of impending danger

During the First Battle of the Marne in 1914, the French army advanced with 72 pigeon lofts

By 1918 there were around 22,000 pigeons carrying post to British soldiers along the western front

The US Army Signal Corps used 600 pigeons in France

A US pigeon called Cher Ami was awarded the French 'Croix de Guerre avec Palme' for delivering 12 important messages during the Battle of Verdun

The final message Cher Ami delivered in October 1918 probably saved the lives 200 US infantrymen. The message was delivered despite the bird being shot

Another famous pigeon to serve American troops was Kaiser. He was captured from the Germans in 1918 during the battle of the Meuse. He was used in the US Army Signal Corps breeding programme and sired over 100 pigeons. Kaiser went on to serve in WW2

During the war in Britain killing, wounding or molesting homing pigeons was punishable under the Defence of the Realm Regulations by six months imprisonment or a £100 fine

A £5 reward was also in place in Britain for any information leading to the conviction of people found guilty of shooting homing pigeons

On 12 September 1918 a young pigeon called 'The Mocker' was sent on a flight carrying important information regarding the location of a

German artillery battery that was destroying an American infantry advance. Despite being wounded in the face (losing an eye), the message was delivered. A few minutes later that German artillery battery was silenced

The Mocker flew 52 missions before being wounded and losing his eye

In March 1918 the British launched a cavalry charge at the German lines. Out of 150 horses used in the charge, only 4 survived the enemy machine-guns

Dogs were very important and carried out many different roles in the trenches, including sniffing out the enemy, carrying supplies; find wounded, raising morale of the troops and delivering messages

When war broke out in 1914, there were no military dogs of any sort attached to the British Army save for one sole Airedale, who served with the 2nd Battalion Norfolk Regiment as a sentry

Germany had 6,000 trained dogs ready for action at the beginning of the war

Because dogs have a superior sense of smell compared to humans they could they could smell oncoming gas attacks before the men in the trenches are were able to alert them in good time to enable gas masks to be put on before the effects of the gas became too great

Lots of dog breeds were used during World War One, but the most popular type of dogs were medium-sized, intelligent and trainable breeds. Doberman Pinschers and German Shepherds were both popular

Doberman's were employed in large numbers by German troops. They were favoured because they are both highly intelligent, easily trainable, and possess excellent guarding abilities.

Many other breeds were used, especially smaller breeds such as terriers, which were most often trained to hunt and kill rats in the trenches

Casualty or 'Mercy' dogs were vital. These dogs were trained to venture out into No Man's Land and search for wounded soldiers. These dogs carried medical supplies on their backs. If a soldier was too badly wounded they would at least have the company of one of these mercy dogs with them in their final moments

Lt-Col. Edwin Hautenville Richardson opened the War Dogs Training School in 1917. It was located in Shoeburyness

Dogs for the WDTS came mostly from Battersea Dogs' Home (then known as the Home for Lost Dogs at Battersea). As demand increased, other dogs' homes in Manchester, Birmingham, Liverpool and Bristol were used

The training of the dogs at Shoeburyness took 5 weeks on average. Lazy or greedy dogs were quickly sent back to their owners

On service, messenger dogs would spent 2 weeks at a time in the trenches

After the war, many of Richardson's trained messenger dogs were retrained as guide dogs for soldiers who'd been rendered blind on service

The work of every British dog on the Western Front, including each run made, distance, destination, the name of the handlers and even the message carried, was recorded in the Central Kennels Register of Dogs and Men. It can be found today in the Imperial War Museum library

Adolf Hitler kept a dog during his time in the trenches

About a million dogs died during the First World War

Because poisoned gas affected animals as well as humans, both dogs and horses had special gas masks developed for them

3,689 horses and miles were safely removed from Gallipoli during the final stage of the British evacuation

The British Mobile Veterinary Section was in effect a Divisional first aid unit providing medical care for sick, wounded or injured horses used by the units of the Division it was attached to

In 1914 a Mobile Veterinary Section was manned by 16 Privates, 1 Shoeing Smith, 1 Corporal, 2 Staff Sergeants, a driver from the Army Service Corps, 2 Batmen and 1 Veterinary Officer

If a horse required greater care that could not be provided by the MVS, the animal would be sent to a Base Veterinary Hospital and its place taken by a horse delivered from ASC Remounts

The war in East Africa claimed approximately 19,000 horses, 11,000 oxen, 10,000 mules, and 2,500 donkeys all of which were killed in service with the British Army

As large amounts of horses and mules were transported out to the war many farmers and workers back in Britain turned to other more exotic animals to help them run their businesses. In Sheffield an Indian elephant called Lizzie was used to cart munitions and scrap metal throughout the city

Camels were also used in Sheffield to help pull heavy loads in the place of horses

Elephants from a local circus were used to plough fields in Surrey

16. CASUALTIES

There were approximately 37,500,000 casualties in total during the war (killed/wounded/missing/prisoner)

230 soldiers perished every hour for the four and a quarter years of conflict

57.6% of all combatants became casualties

There were an estimated 8.5 million combatants killed from all nations during the war

Approximately 7.5 million soldiers who died in WW1 have no known grave

Approximately 7 million combatants were maimed for life but survived

Approximately 21 million soldiers were wounded in one way or another on all sides

80,000 British army soldiers suffered from shell shock over the course of the war. That's approximately 2% of the men who were called up for active service

Around 8 million civilians were killed during the war from non-influenza causes

132 British sailors were killed on 6 August 1914 when HMS *Amphion* sunk after hitting a German mine in the English Channel. They were the first British casualties of the war

World War 1 trench warfare was so intense that 10% of all the soldiers who fought were killed. That's more than double the percentage of fighting soldiers who were killed in the Second World War (4.5%)

At the end of the war there were over 250,000 wounded British soldiers who suffered total or partial amputation

Of all British soldiers mobilised, 33.67% were killed or wounded

Of all French soldiers mobilised, 67.9% were killed or wounded

During the course of the war, 11% of France's entire population were killed or wounded

Millions of soldiers suffered 'shell shock', or post traumatic stress disorder, due to the horrors of trench warfare

Approximate figures of total battle deaths:
- Germany - 1.8 million
- Russia - 1.7 million
- France - 1.3 million
- Austria-Hungary - 1.2 million
- Britain - 880,000
- Italy - 650,00
- Turkey - 325,000
- Bulgaria – 87,500
- India - 72,000
- Canada - 65,000
- Australia - 62,000
- USA – 116,000
- New Zealand - 18,000

•South Africa - 9,300

Britain's losses (deaths) in WW1 were approximately 230% higher than those in WW2

Aircrew casualties (killed/missing/wounded/prisoner)
- Britain & Commonwealth - 16, 620
- Germany - 16,050
- France - 7,250
- USA - 513

Naval casualties (killed/wounded)
- Britain & Commonwealth - 39,160
- Germany - 78,300
- France – 15,650
- Italy - 8,420
- USA - 8,106
- Austria-Hungary - 1,290

Allied forces suffered a combined 12.6 million wounded soldiers

The central powers suffered a combined 8.4 million wounded soldiers

Allied forces lost 4.1 million men as prisoners of war. The Central Powers lost approximately 3.5 million prisoners

There were 863 British and Commonwealth deaths on 11 November 1918

The last British battle casualty of the war is believed to be L/12643 Private George Ellison, 5th (Royal Irish) Lancers. He was killed on 11 November 1918 aged 25

The last man believed killed in the Great War was US Army Private Henry Gunther, he was killed 60 seconds before the 11th hour

The single biggest loss of life from a U-boat strike was on the Italian troopship *Principe Umberto* which was sunk on 8 June 1916 with the loss of 1,750 lives

On 22 September 1914 German U-Boats sank 3 British ships (*Aboukir*, *Cressy* and *Houge*) with the loss of 1,400 sailors

In December 1914 the Germany Navy bombarded the English coastal towns of Scarborough, Hartlepool and Whitby, killing 18 civilians.

From a total population of about 5 million, Australia contributed 322,000 men to the Allied war effort, of whom approximately 280,000 were casualties, the highest rate of loss of any combatant in the war

6,840 German flying personnel were killed

The 1918 Spanish influenza epidemic in 1918 accounted for a minimum of 21.5 million deaths

Allied Western Front casualties during 1914 totalled approximately 1,140,000, with France accounting for 995,000 of those

German Western Front casualties during August – November 1914 totalled approximately 677,440

On the Eastern Front in 1914 German and Austrian losses amounted to 1.27 million men

Russian casualties on the Eastern Front in 1914 was 1.8 million men. 486,000 were taken prisoner

Allied casualties in Eastern, Western and South Africa during 1914 totalled 2,982. German casualties in the same regions were 798 with another 2,273 prisoners taken

On the Western Front in 1915 the French lost 966,687 casualties (killed, missing and wounded) with the British losing 296,583 men

In 1915 on the Western Front the German army suffered 652,270 casualties

On the Italian Front during 1915 Italy suffered 278,500 losses (22,500 PoWs) with Austria losing 165,000 men (30,000 PoWs)

In 1915 on the Eastern Front Russia suffered almost 2,500,000 casualties (over 1 million prisoners)

Also on the Eastern Front in 1915 Austrian and German losses combined were over 960,000 killed, missing, wounded and prisoner

In 1916 the Allies lost 1,535,246 men along with 3,500 field guns, 16 tanks and c1,500 aircraft on the Western Front

Germany lost 962,488 casualties in 1916 on the Western Front along with c1,912 field guns, over 1,000 machine guns and c500 aircraft

During 1916 Germany and Austria suffered 1.35 million casualties including over 500,000 Prisoners of War

Russia suffered 2.4 million casualties on the Eastern Front in 1916, including over 340,000 Prisoners of War

The first Italian casualty was Riccardo Di Giusto who was killed in the early hours of 24 May 1915

From May to October 1915, the Italian Army suffered over 150,000 and another 60,000 dead. This was almost one quarter of her mobilized forces

On 13 December 1916 10,000 Italian soldiers were killed by avalanches in the Dolomites. It was to become known as 'White Friday'

It is estimated that shellfire exploding in the rocky terrain of the Italian front caused 70% more casualties per rounds expended than on the soft ground of Belgium and France

L/141916 Private John Parr, 4th Battalion, the Middlesex Regiment, is generally considered to be the first British soldier to die on the

Western Front when he was killed while on patrol near Obourg

The Field Ambulance of the First World War was not a vehicle. It was a mobile camp of the Royal Army Medical Corps situated close behind the front lines and was set up to receive wounded and sick men from the front

The job of the Field Ambulance was to treat men who could be quickly returned to unit (the lightly wounded or sick) but in general to prepare the men for a move to a Casualty Clearing Station

In 1914, each British infantry Division had 3 Field Ambulances, comprising of 10 officers and 224 men per Field Ambulance

The Field Ambulances relied heavily on horses for transport. The typical Field Ambulance possessed 14 riding horses and 52 pack horses to carry the various wagons and water carts

A Field Ambulance would also have a single bicycle

By the end of 1914, each Field Ambulance also had 7 motor ambulances

The officers and men of the British Field Ambulance carried no weapons or ammunition

Over the course of the war approximately 50,000 British officers were evacuated back to England suffering from sickness

Over the course of the war approximately 950,000 British rank and file soldiers were evacuated back to England suffering from sickness

Each British soldier was given 2 bandages as part of their field dressing kit. This was to enable them to treat a bullet wound that passed completely through their body – thus causing 2 wounds

By the time the US Army entered the war, shell shock was beginning to be studied. The US were at the forefront of this study and even had psychologists at the front as part of their medical teams

17. SURRENDER, ARMISTICE & PEACE TREATIES

The term 'Armistice' means a cessation of hostilities as a prelude to peace negotiations

In the context of the First World War 'the armistice' is generally referred to in context of the agreement between the Germans and the Allies to end the war on 11 November 1918

There were 3 separate armistices signed towards the end of the war: Turkey signed an armistice on 30 October 1918, Austria-Hungary signed one on 3 November, and finally, Germany signed an armistice on 11 November 1918

On 29 October 1918 the Australian Imperial authorities asked Italy for an armistice, but the Italians continued to advance, reaching Trento, Udine, and Trieste

On 3 November 1918 Austria-Hungary sent a flag of truce to the Italian Commander to ask again for an armistice and terms of peace

The terms of peace for the Italian front were arranged by telegraph with the Allied Authorities in Paris communicating terms to the Austrian Commander. They were quickly accepted

The Armistice with Austria was signed in the Villa Giusti, near Padua, on 3 November, and took effect on 4 November 1918 at 3pm

Austria and Hungary signed separate armistices following the overthrow of the Habsburg Monarchy and the collapse of the Austro-Hungarian Empire

The war on the Eastern Front was brought to a close in December 1917 (and followed by the Treaty of Brest-Litovsk), as was Romania's war (resulting in the Treaty of Bucharest)

After the Russian revolution of October 1917 Russia was in no position to continue the fight. Armistice negotiations commenced on 3 December 1917 and a general ceasefire across the Eastern Front came into being on 16 December 1917

Peace talks between the Central Powers and the Bolsheviks took place 6 days later

The Treaty of Brest-Litovsk was signed by the Central Powers and the Bolsheviks on 3 March 1918

The Treaty of Brest-Litovsk relieved Russia of approximately 30% of its imperial population. Poland, Finland, Latvia, Lithuania, Estonia, Ukraine and Belorussia all moved under German influence under the terms of the agreement

The Treaty of Brest-Litovsk was very pro-German and caused resentment in Austria-Hungary and Bulgaria

The Treaty of Brest-Litovsk was formally annulled as part of the Armistice agreement between the Allies and the Central Powers on 11 November 1918

The collapse of Russia on the Eastern Front persuaded Romania to sign an armistice with the Central Powers and the Treaty of Bucharest was signed on 9 December 1917

The Treaty of Bucharest was ripped up by Romania when they re-entered the war on 10 November 1918 and formally annulled one day later when the Armistice was signed on 11 November 1918

Germany initiated peace negotiations with the USA on 4 October 1918

On 10 November a German delegation met Allied military representatives in the forest of Compiègne to conclude peace talks and sign an armistice

The armistice was signed in the morning of 11 November in Froch's railway carriage

Fighting officially ending at 11am on 11 November 1918

The original peace treaty signed by Germany on 11 November was only actually valid for 30 days but was continually renewed until the signing of the Treaty of Versailles

The Treaty of Versailles was the formal peace settlement signed after the war had ended

The Treaty was signed in the vast Versailles Palace near Paris, hence its name

The Treaty was eventually signed and ratified on 29 June 1919

27 victorious powers signed the Treaty of Versailles

The terms of the Treaty were dominated by the wishes of the 'Big Three': David Lloyd George (Britain) Georges Clemenceau (France) and Woodrow Wilson (USA)

US President Woodrow Wilson set out America's view of post-war peace on 8 January 1918 when he outlined his 'Fourteen Points' to congress

On 4 October 1918, Germany started to talk to the USA (not France or Britain) about initiating peace talks. The Germans were keen to conclude a peace based upon Wilson's Fourteen Points

Although somewhat controversial, by November 1918 they had formed the basis of surrender terms for Germany

Germany was forced to surrender 5,000 artillery pieces, 30,000 machine guns, 2,000 aircraft, 5,000 locomotives, 150,000 railway wagons, 3,000 minenwerfers and its entire submarine fleet– the British Navy received 176 U-boats

The size of the German army allowed under the terms of the Treaty of Versailles was 100,000 men of all ranks

A major potential stumbling block to peace was Wilson's insistence upon the abdication of the German Kaiser, Wilhelm II

On 8 November a German delegation met with Allied Supreme Commander Ferdinand Foch – who was to lead the military negotiations – in the forest of Compiegne, some 65km north-east of Paris

With Germany actively seeking an armistice and revolution threatening, calls for Kaiser Wilhelm II to abdicate grew in intensity

Wilhelm's abdication was announced by Chancellor Prince Max von Baden in a 9 November 1918 proclamation – before the Kaiser had in fact consented to abdicate

In the wake of the Kaiser's abdication his eldest son – Crown Prince Wilhelm –expressed a desire on 11 November 1918 – the date of the armistice – to be allowed to lead his army back home to Germany. His wish was rejected

After his abdication the Kaiser and the Crown Prince went into exile in Holland

The Kaiser's abdication proclamation was formally published in Berlin on 30 November 1918

The Armistice began at on 11 November 1918 at 11am (French time)

– the eleventh hour of the eleventh day of the eleventh month. The Armistice itself was agreed 6 hours earlier at 5am with the first term of it being that fighting would end at 11am.

The signing of the Armistice took place in Ferdinand Foch's railway carriage in the Forest of Compiègne, about 37 miles (60km) north of Paris. The location was chosen as it was remote and discreet

In 1940, another armistice was signed in the very same railway carriage in the very same Forest of Compiègne. This time it was Germany forcing France to sign surrender and Armistice terms during the Second World War

Adolf Hitler sat in the same seat that Ferdinand Foch used in 1918

After the 1940 Armistice and surrender documents were signed, the carriage was taken and exhibited in Germany, but was destroyed in 1945

If Germany broke any of the terms of the Armistice, such as not evacuating areas they were ordered to evacuate, not handing over weapons or prisoners of war in the timescales given or causing damage to any individual or their property, fighting would begin again with 48 hours' notice

Germany was ordered to provide information about the location of mines or traps they had placed and reveal what other things they had deliberately destroyed or caused damage too (such as polluting or poisoning springs or wells)

By signing the Armistice and the Treaty of Versailles, Germany was made to accept the blame for the First World War and forced to pay reparations for the damage caused, estimated to total about £22 billion ($35 billion, €27 billion) in current money. It was only in 2010 that Germany paid off its war debt, with a final payment of £59 million ($95 million, €71 million)

In September 1919 Austria-Hungary signed the Treaty of St Germain

In August 1920 the Ottoman Empire signed the Treaty of Sevres

British public opinion in November 1918 was that the Armistice of 11 November was premature and that the Allies should have either forced German surrender in the field or driven them back in Germany

Germany herself continued to insist that her armies had not been beaten and the request for an Armistice was purely to save any more bloodshed

Peaceful evacuation of German occupied territories on the Western Front was required within 14 days

Allied forced occupied the left bank of the Rhine within a month of the Armistice, with a neutral zone set upon the right side

At the end of the war, the Allies occupied Constantinople (Istanbul) and the Ottoman government collapsed

The Treaty of Sèvres, a plan designed by the Allies to divide up the remaining Ottoman territories, was signed on 10 August 1920, although it was never ratified by the Sultan

Although China was part of the Allied contingent, she ended up losing territory after the war, with Jiaozhou Bay and most of Shandong in north China forcibly given to Japan

China did not sign the Treaty of Versailles, instead signing a separate peace treaty with Germany in 1921

French Field Marshal Ferdinand Foch, who was of the opinion the restrictions on Germany didn't go far enough, said of the Treaty of Versailles, 'This is not Peace. It is an Armistice for twenty years.'

18. REMEMBRANCE

Armistice Day, Remembrance Day or Veterans Day is commemorated in many countries involved in the First World War on 11 November every year or on the Sunday nearest to it (or, as is becoming more common, on both days)

In the United Kingdom, Remembrance Day ceremonies have been televised every year since 1946, although the first live broadcast was in 1937

The first version of the Whitehall Cenotaph – made from timber and plaster was unveiled on 19 July 1919

The largest of the Messines Ridge 1917 mine craters (Spanbroekmolen) is now the Pool of Peace. The pool is 27 metres deep and has a diameter of 129 metres

Marshall Joffre issued an order in March 1915 banning exhumations for the period of the war, but despite this many British families, especially more wealthy ones, continued to insist on their sons/husbands be removed and reburied in Britain

Finally, in an effort to put a stop to the exhumation of bodies, Major General Neville Macready, Adjutant-General to the British Expeditionary Force issued an order forbidding exhumation on account, 'of the difficulties of treating impartially the claims by persons of different social standing'

Major General Fabien Ware was originally a member of the British Red Cross but was later put in charge of meticulously recording the graves of fallen Allied soldiers in France and Belgium

Originally when a grave was recorded by Ware and his team the family would receive a photo of the cross along with instructions of the grave location

By October 1915, the new Graves Registration Commission ran by Ware had over 31,000 graves registered, and 50,000 by May 1916

So successful was this service that Commission was quickly extended to other theatres of war including Salonika, Greece, Egypt and Mesopotamia

On 21 May 1917 the Imperial War Graves Commission was created by Royal Charter

The Prince of Wales was the first President of the IWGC with Lord Derby its chairman. Ware was Vice Chairman and Macready was also on the board

The Imperial War Graves Commission was charged to care for all members of the Armed Forces of the British Empire who, 'died from wounds inflicted, accident occurring or disease contracted, whole on active service whether on sea or land'

Qualification for burial in an IWGC cemetery after the war was that a man or woman had to had been a member of the armed service between 4 August 1914 and 31 August 1921

Between the Armistice and September 1921, special Graves Concentration Units carried out systematic searches of the Western Front searching for remote graves. During this time they found 204,650 bodies and reburied them in special cemeteries set aside for them

To ensure all areas of the Empire were represented, the High Commissioners for Canada, Australia, New Zealand, South Africa, India and Newfoundland were also represented on the board of the new Commission

Rudyard Kipling was appointed literary advisor to the IWGC towards the end of October 1917

The first meeting of the IWGC was in November 1917. Many of the major principles that were ratified in that meeting are still upheld today

The IWGC was renamed the Commonwealth War Graves Commission in 1960

The first Commission memorial to be unveiled was the Menin Gate in Ypres in July 1927

At 8pm every evening, the road that passes under the Menin Gate in Ypres is closed to traffic to allow the sounding of the Last Post by local buglers

By 9 July 2015 the Last Post would have been played 30,000 times under the Menin Gate in Ypres

It was Major General Neville Macready who insisted that memorials and graves should carry no distinction between officers and men. This was a big departure from the previous wars where the ordinary soldier tended to be buried in a mass grave

The largest memorial to the missing is Thiepval Memorial. It carries the names of 72,116 officers and men who became casualties during the Battle of the Somme and who have no known grave

The Thiepval Memorial in France, stands at over 45 metres high

The Commission cares for the graves and memorials of almost 1.7 million Commonwealth servicemen and women who died in the 2 world wars. These include the graves of more than 935,000 identified casualties and almost 212,000 unidentified individuals. The names of almost 760,000 people can be found on memorials to the missing

Most CWGC headstones are made from a white limestone called Portland stone

All headstones are of a uniform shape and size: 2 foot 6 inches high, 1 foot 3 inches wide and 3 inches thick with an emphasis on simplicity with clear lettering to cut costs to a minimum and help with future maintenance

The gentle curving of the top of the headstone was designed to help disperse rain and stop water pouring down the front of the headstone, thus minimising water damage

The lettering used on all headstones and memorials has chosen so it could be read at a 45 degree angle from above and the side, so visitors didn't need to kneel down to read any inscriptions

The inscriptions, including the regimental crests were engraved into the headstones by a hand-guided machine called a pantograph

Between 1920 and 1923 more than 4,000 headstones were shipped to France each week

Cemeteries with more than 40 graves have a Cross of Sacrifice. Made of Portland stone it stands on an octagonal block. The cross itself has a bronze sword pointing towards to the ground in its centre

The Cross of Sacrifice was designed by Sir Reginald Bloomfield. He designed it so it could be produced in four different sizes, meaning smaller cemeteries could carry one that fitted

Cemeteries with over 400 graves often have 'The Stone of Remembrance' as well as the 'Cross of Sacrifice'. The stone is made out of Portland stone and is 12 feet in length, lying raised upon three steps. Inscribed on the stone are the words 'Their Name Liveth For Evermore'

The Stone of Remembrance was designed by Sir Edwin Lutyens

This inscription, carved into every Stone of Remembrance was chosen by Rudyard Kipling

In all but the smallest cemeteries there is a register, which is often found in a bronze register box, often built into the wall of the cemetery near the gate or entrance. Within the register is a list of all the names of the soldiers buried in that cemetery. A visitor book is also available for visitors to write comments about their trip

The largest CWGC cemetery is 'Tyne Cot' in Belgium. It contains 11,956 graves from the First World War. 8,369 of these are un-named as it has been impossible to identify the body buried in those graves. On each of these headstones is written 'A Soldier of the Great War. Known unto God'. This epitaph was penned by Rudyard Kipling.

The Tyne Cot memorial to the missing lists 34,953 officers and men and is one of 4 memorials to the missing covering the area on the Western Front known as the Ypres Salient

The largest Commonwealth War Graves Commission cemetery in Britain is Brookwood Military Cemetery in Surrey, which contains the graves of over 5,000 servicemen and women in 37 acres of ground

On the Gallipoli peninsular there are 31 war cemeteries containing 22,000 graves

Out of the 22,000 war graves on the Gallipoli peninsula, only 9,000 come with named headstones

The ANZAC Bridge in Sydney was christened as such on Remembrance Day in 1998 to honour the memory of the ANZACS. An Australian flag flies atop the eastern pylon and a New Zealand flag flies atop the western pylon

Fromelles (Pheasant Wood) Military Cemetery in France is the newest Commission cemetery – dedicated in 2010

The Commonwealth War Graves Commission has an online database that lists the names and place of commemoration of the 1.7 million men and women of the Commonwealth forces who died during the two world wars. It can be found at www.cwgc.org

Germany set up her own war graves commission (Volksbund Deutsche Kriegsgräberfürsorge) after the war to ensure the maintenance and upkeep of German war graves in Europe and North Africa

The German War Graves Commission was set up initially as a charity on 16 December 1919 in accordance with Article 225 of the Treaty of Versailles

With 47,864 burials the Menen Germany War Cemetery in Flanders is the largest WW1 German war cemetery on the Western Front

The largest WW1 German war cemetery in France is the Neuville-St Vaast German War Cemetery near Arras with 44,833 burials

The Langemark German War Cemetery is situated near the battle grounds of the First Battle of Ypres and holds the remains of more than 44,000 Germans soldiers. There is a mass 'comrades grave' containing the remains of 24,917 servicemen including the famous air 'Ace' Werner Voss

Established by Congress in 1923, the American Battle Monuments Commission (ABMC) manages 24 overseas military cemeteries, and 26 memorials, monuments, and markers. Nearly all the cemeteries and memorials specifically honour those who served in World War I or World War II

The largest American war cemetery is the Meuse-Argonne American Cemetery and Memorial in France with 14,246 burials within the 130 acre site and another 954 names on the Tablets of the Missing

19. AFTERMATH

4 empires collapsed after WWI: Ottoman, Austro-Hungarian, German, and Russian

When the war ended in November 1918, 8.4 million women were granted the right to vote

The naval blockade of Germany continued in place after the Armistice up until the signing of the Treaty of Versailles on 28 June 1919

It is claimed that a quarter of a million Germans died due to sickness or starvation in the 8 month period of blockade that followed the end of the war

The terms of the Armistice did allow food to be shipped in to Germany but it had to be shipped in by German shipping

An Allied taskforce was set up in early 1919 to help feed Germany and by May 1919 Germany was receiving significant American and Allied food shipments

After WWI, Finland, Estonia, Latvia, Lithuania, the Tsardom of Poland and Ukraine all became independent nations after the collapse of the Russian empire

First World War guns were fired announcing the formal notice of the birth of the Duke and Duchess of Cambridge's baby son on 22 July 2013

King Albert of Belgium re-entered Brussels on 22 November 1918 and put in place a plan for rapid economic recovery and reconstruction

As US troops returned home after the war it was feared that the African American contingent would start to demand equality with white Americans. Racial tension shot through the roof with race riots erupting in twenty-six cities across America

The Armistice signed on 11 November 1918 did not bring immediate peace to Europe. Fresh fighting broke out soon afterwards in Russia and the former Austria-Hungary, mostly due to territorial demands of the newly independent states such as Poland

The war cost the Italian government more money than it had spent in the previous 50 years – and Italy had only been in the war three years

Italy got very little reward from the Treaty of Versailles. The Italian public believed that her leaders there had been humiliated and generally ignored by America, France and Britain. They were right as the Italian delegation were mostly ignored. This heaped further humiliation on the government. For Italian nationalists the failure of the government to stand up to the 'Big Three' was unforgivable

4 years after the war, after an attempted communist revolution, Mussolini and his blackshirts marched on Rome and took power

Austria was forbidden to make a political connection with Germany

The former Ottoman Empire was reinvented as Turkey, and limited to a region around Istanbul and Central Anatolia. These limits, however, were not recognised by Turkish nationalists, who would later extend Turkish holdings with a military victory over the Greeks in 1919

After the war the Statute of the League of Nations was adopted by the victors in April 1919

Following the end of World War I and the abdication of the Kaiser, Germany attempted to reinvent herself by forming the Weimar Republic (named after the town where the new constitution was written), a democratic federal republic, governed by a president and parliament

The democratic government of Germany was declared in February 1919 at the small town of Weimar. It was too dangerous to make a declaration in Berlin where there had just been a revolt by a Communist group called the Spartacists

Many Germans associated the new democracy with defeat and did not believe the new system would provide the strong leadership they had been used to with the Kaiser. As a result there were few people in Germany that were loyal to the Weimar Republic

The Republic's first President, Friedrich Ebert, signed the new German constitution into law on 11 August 1919. The constitution is named after Weimar although it was signed into law by Friedrich Ebert in Schwarzburg. This is due to the fact that Ebert was on holiday in Schwarzburg, while the parliament working out the constitution was gathered in Weimar

For the soldiers who came back from the trenches, they received a pack of civilian clothes, some medals and a small cash payment. The average British Tommy received the equivalent of a couple of weeks wages, officers got slightly more

Sir Douglas Haig become Earl Haig after the war and received £100,000 after the war as a thank you from the country. A massive sum of money at that time

After leaving the army in 1920 Haig devoted his time to trying to improve the welfare of ex-servicemen and was instrumental in the formation of the British Legion in June 1921

The 1918 flu pandemic that spread across the globe in 1918 infected over 500 million people and killed between 50 and 100 million people

To maintain wartime morale British censors limited the reporting of the deaths in the warring nations of Britain, France, America and

Germany. However they were freer to report the effects of the flu in neutral Spain. As a result the pandemic was known as 'Spanish Flu'

In many cities in America, returning veterans who had disfiguring wounds from the war were required to cover up and wear hoods in public in case they scared women and children

In Chicago if a disfigured soldier did not cover up they could be charged with 'Being ugly on the public way'

Following the Armistice many of the Allied troops were not repatriated back home immediately with a large number following the German army back into Germany where they took on occupational duties. There was also the small matter of clearing the battlefields

Unlike France, which imposed its first income tax to pay for the war, the German Kaiser and Parliament decided to fund the war entirely by borrowing

The exchange rate of the mark against the US dollar fell steadily throughout the war from 4.2 to 8.91 marks per dollar

It was the territories of France and Belgium that bore the brunt of the fighting during the war; as a result Germany had come out of the war with most of its industrial power intact, and was arguably in a better position to return to its pre-war economic strength than many of the Allies

In an effort to curb potential German economic growth, the 'London ultimatum' of May 1921 demanded reparations in gold or foreign currency to be paid in annual instalments of 2,000,000,000 (2 billion) goldmarks plus 26% of the value of Germany's exports

Because war reparations were required to be repaid in gold or foreign currency and not their own currency, Germany started to mass-print bank notes to buy foreign currency which was in turn used to pay reparations- greatly affecting inflation rates

Between 1921 and 1923 Germany suffered from hyperinflation

In 1922, the highest denomination was 50,000 marks. By 1923, the highest denomination was 100,000,000,000,000 marks

In December 1923 the exchange rate was 4,200,000,000,000 German marks to 1 US dollar

In the United Kingdom, funding the war had a severe economic cost. From being the world's largest overseas investor, it suddenly found itself with massive debts to pay, with interest payments forming around 40% of all government spending

Those men that fought in the war became known as the 'Lost Generation' because they never fully recovered from their suffering

The 1921 United Kingdom census found 19,803,022 women and 18,082,220 men in England and Wales, a difference of 1.72 million which newspapers called the 'Surplus Two Million'

Each year Belgian and French farmers plough up large quantities of shells, barbed wire, ammunitions, shrapnel and trench remnants from their fields. This is called the 'iron harvest'

The French Département du Déminage (Department of Mine Clearance) recovers about 900 tons of unexploded munitions every year

Since 1945, approximately 630 French clearers have died handling unexploded munitions

After each iron harvest many of the shells were simply dumped into the sea, although this practice stopped in 1980

REFERENCES

1914-1918: The History of the First World War by David Stevenson (Penguin, 2004)

1918: A Very British Victory (Weidenfeld & Nicholson, 2008)

Battle Story: Gallipoli 1915 by Peter Doyle (The History Press, 2011)

British Tommy 1914-18 by Martin Pegler and Mike Chappell (Osprey, 2008)

Chronicle of the First World War - Volumes 1 & 2 by Randal Gray (Facts on File, 1991)

First World War by Martin Gilbert (Harper Collins, 1994)

For Conspicuous Gallantry... Winners of the Military Cross and Bar during the Great War (Vol 1) by Scott Addington (Matador, 2006)

French Poilu 1914-18 by Ian Sumner (Osprey, 2009)

Gallipoli by Peter Hart (Profile Books, 2011)

Passchendaele: The Sacrificial Ground by Nigel Steel and Peter Hart (Phoenix, 2001)

Somme by Peter Hart (Weidenfeld & Nicolson, 2005)

The Australian Army in World War 1 by Robert Fleming & Mike Chappell (Osprey, 2012)

The 'Baby Killers'. German Air Raids on Britain in the First World War by Thomas Fegan (Pen and Sword Military, 2012)

The British Army 1914-18 by D S V Fosten & R J Marrion (Osprey, 2008)

The British Army in World War I (3 - The Eastern Fronts) by Mike Chappel (Osprey, 2005)

The Eastern Front 1914-1917 by Norman Stone (London, 1975)

The First Day on the Somme by Martin Middlebrook (Military Book Society, 1971)

The First World War by John Keegan (Hutchinson London, 1999)

The German Army 1914-18 by D S V Fosten & R J Marrion (Osprey, 2008)

The Guns of August by Barbara W. Tuchman (Presido Press, 2004)

The Italian Army of World War 1 by David Nicolle (Osprey, 2003)

The Macmillan Dictionary of the First World War by Stephen Pope and Elizabeth-Anne Wheal (Macmillan, 1995)

The New Zealand Expeditionary Force in World War 1 by Wayne Stack & Mike Chappell (Osprey, 2011)

The Price of Glory: Verdun 1916 by Alistair Horne (Penguin, 1993)

The Russian Army 1914-18 by Nik Cornish (Osprey, 2001)

The Russian Revolution 1899-1919 by Richard Pipes (Collins Harvill,

1990)

The US Army of World War I by Mark R Henry and Stephen Walsh (Osprey, 2003)

The World War One Source Book by P.J. Haythornthwaite (Arms and Armour Press, 1996)

Tommy: The British Soldier on the Western Front by Richard Holmes (Harper Perennial 2005)

Trench Talk by Peter Doyle & Julian Walker (Spellmount, 2012)

US Doughboy 1916-19 by Thomas A Hoff and Adam Hook (Osprey, 2005)

World War 1 Fact Book by William Van der Kloot (Amberley Publishing Plc, 2010)

World War One: A Short History by Norman Stone (Penguin, 2008)

World War One: A Layman's Guide by Scott Addington (Independently published, 2012)

Ypres: The First Battle 1914 by Ian F.W. Beckett (Pearson Longman, 2006)

ABOUT THE AUTHOR

Scott Addington runs Military Research UK, a company specialising in uncovering family heroes and has always been fascinated by individual stories of war and battle. This intrigue lead him to find out more about the men behind the medals in books such as 'For Conspicuous Gallantry...' and the soon to be published 'Britain's Bravest Soldiers - The First World War'.

As well as the personal stories, Scott is on a mission to open up the First World War to children, teenagers and adults alike who would not necessarily read 900 page epics on the subject. To this end he wrote 'World War One: A Layman's Guide' which is a perfect introduction to the subject and his 'The Great War 100' project of telling the story of the First World War using infographics aims to open the subject up to a whole new audience when it is launched in 2014.

In 2009, Scott cycled the entire Western Front trench line system (550 miles) raising several thousand pounds for the Royal British Legion's Poppy Appeal. You can read all about this adventure in the charity ebook 'Heroes of The Line'. In 2014 he plans to do another ride for charity, this time even longer and more crazy than the last one.

You can follow Scott on Twitter: @military_search

Printed in Great Britain
by Amazon